MW00461510

fRienos in the LORO

the Family Rosary Mission Statement

In the spirit of our founder, Father Patrick Peyton, CSC, and under the sponsorship of the Congregation of Holy Cross, The Family Rosary and Family Theater Productions serve Jesus Christ and his Church throughout the world by promoting and supporting the spiritual well-being of the family.

Faithful to Mary, the Mother of God, The Family Rosary encourages family prayer, especially the Rosary.

Family Theater Productions directs its efforts to the evangelization of culture, using mass media to entertain, inspire and educate families.

Holy Cross Family Ministries
518 Washington Street
North Easton, MA 02356
(800) 299 PRAY

web site: www.hcfm.org

Email: mission@familyrosary.org
Web Site: http://www.familyrosary.org

fRiends in the LoRd

Exploring Consecrated Discipleship

Thomas Feeley, CSC

BOOKS & MEDIA
Boston

Library of Congress Cataloging in Publication Data:

Feeley, Thomas.
   Friends in the Lord : Exploring Consecrated Discipleship /
Thomas Feeley.
         p.   cm.
   ISBN 0-8198-2672-3 (pbk.)
   1.   Monastic and religious life. 2.   Spiritual life—Catholic
Church.
   I. Title.
   BX2435 .F365 2001
   255—dc21

                                                        2001002599

ISBN 0-8198-2672-3

Printed and published in the U.S.A. by Pauline Books & Media,
50 Saint Pauls Avenue, Boston MA 02130-3491.

www.pauline.org

Pauline Books & Media is the publishing house of the Daughters
of St. Paul, an international congregation of women religious
serving the Church with the communications media.

1 2 3 4 5 6 7   06 05 04 03 02 01

Dedication

I dedicate this book to those men who, responding to Christ's call, are preparing to commit themselves to live as **Friends in the Lord** with the priests and brothers of the Congregation of Holy Cross.

I offer it in memory of my mother, who first taught me by word and example to be a **Friend of the Lord** and whom God called to himself in the ninety-fifth year of her life on December 2, 1996.

Contents

Preface

The past three decades have witnessed great changes in consecrated life as well as in our understanding of the Church and the Sacred Scriptures. Some of the themes articulated here were first developed in retreats I gave to religious communities to help them adapt to those changes and still preserve what is truly fundamental in religious life.

In writing this book I decided to forego telling stories and using real-life examples (which readers can easily supply from their own experience) and to rely instead on Sacred Scripture. I have taken great pains to indicate Scriptural references, and I strongly recommend that readers pray over the passages referenced. For we are told: "All scripture is inspired by God and is useful for teaching, for reproof, for correction, and for training in righteousness, so that everyone who belongs to God may be proficient, equipped for every good work" (2 Tim 3:16–17). If this book inspires its readers to read the Scriptures meditatively, then I think the effort expended in writing it will be amply justified.

This volume looks at religious life from the perspective of love, the one commandment of the Lord. For love, like the love Christ has for us, is the heart of the Christian life and of the consecrated life as well. While religious take vows of poverty, chastity, and obedience, all Christians are called to observe the spirit of the evangelical counsels according to their own state of life. For chastity, poverty, and obedience are ways to free our hearts for a total dedication to the Lord. Religious live in community to support one another in their individual and communal striving to love selflessly like Christ, while most Christians live out this way of love in their families. Such Christlike love gives meaning to all we do in our lives and provides the clearest witness that God is in our midst.

My sincere gratitude is due to Wendy Hanawalt, who with great skill and diligence typed the original manuscript, and to Dorothy Halloran, who with unfailing patience and kindness made successive modifications to it.

Feast of Our Lady of Lourdes
February 11, 1999
Stonehill College

I

fRienos in the LoRo

OW CAN WE KNOW WHAT GOD IS LIKE? WE HAVE NEVER seen God, and left to ourselves we hardly know what to make of him. But Jesus Christ, the Son of God, told us that God wants us to worship him "in spirit and truth" (Jn 4:23). Jn us taught us to approach God as children turn to their parents: with joy, affection, trust, and sincerity. For as good fathers and mothers completely dedicate themselves to their children's welfare, so God cares about us. "God so loved the world that he gave his only Son, so that everyone who believes in him may not perish but may have eternal life" (Jn 3:16). Christ, therefore, taught us to call God "Father."

But Christ uses another analogy to express his perfect love for us: he calls us his "friends." How can friendship express divine love, and how can this kind of love influence our religious life in community?

In the past, friendships between religious were often regarded with suspicion. The close bonds that developed between friends were seen as pulling them apart from and fragmenting the whole community. Some friendships can be divisive, but they need not be. Christ even presents the friendship he has for us as the ideal we must imitate.

In its most basic sense, love is the conscious tending to what we judge to be good. There are two basic types of love, acquisitive and appreciative, and two corresponding types of friendship.

Acquisitive love arises from a physical need, such as hunger or thirst, which grows stronger as long as the need is not met. But once the need is met, desire ceases. After a good meal, for example, we forget about food and turn our attention to other things. Notice that love or desire for what meets our physical needs is a desire for a material thing, which must be possessed before it can be used, and once used, is gone. Such a desire based on need is self-centered; we seek something simply to satisfy our needs, not for its own sake.

But appreciative love is not based on need but on our insight into beauty. The beautiful pleases and delights us simply by being contemplated. We need not possess the object in order to enjoy it, and many people can enjoy it without it being used up, as in an experience of viewing paintings in an art museum. Once the beautiful has been experienced, it awakens love and desire, which grow stronger the more we appreciate something. The object loved and admired in this way is not treated as a means but as an end in itself, for its beauty commands our admiration. Whether a sunset or a painting, something beautiful makes us forget ourselves and turn our attention to the beauty before us. Such appreciative love is self-transcending.

These two types of love can help us understand friendships. True friendship is benevolent love and arises when two people seek the good of one another. There are different types of friendship, depending on how much of ourselves we put into the relationship. In some friendships, such as an amicable business partnership, both partners sincerely seek each other's good, for they will each profit from the other's success. Each needs the advantage that the other can provide. These friendships are based on mutual needs and usually last only as long as the relationship fills a need. Such friendships tend to be more self-centered than selfless.

But deeper friendships are based on a sincere love that sees the true good of the other person. As we discover this goodness, we are drawn to love the other person. True friends appreciate and understand each other. Because they may have the same ideals and moral commitments, true friends base their relationship not on mutual needs but on a sincere, selfless love for the other. Such friendships endure and grow deeper and more satisfying with time. Sincere friends have common interests. As they spend time together doing what both enjoy, they enrich each other by generously sharing their gifts. They give with no thought of getting something in return.

We cherish such close friendships because they don't often come into our lives, and they take time to develop. Persons reveal themselves gradually, in various and sometimes difficult situations. It takes time to get to know another person very well. We cannot be close friends with everyone. Yet despite these limitations and because sincere friendships show forth such selfless, generous, joyful, and stable love, Christ uses friendship as an analogy for the kind of love he has for us. Thus at the Last Supper he tells the apostles:

> As the Father has loved me, so I have loved you; abide in my love. If you keep my commandments, you will abide in my love, just as I have kept my Father's commandments and abide in his love. I have said these things to

you so that my joy may be in you, and that your joy may be complete.

This is my commandment, that you love one another as I have loved you. No one has greater love than this, to lay down one's life for one's friends. You are my friends if you do what I command you. I do not call you servants any longer, because the servant does not know what the master is doing; but I have called you friends, because I have made known to you everything that I have heard from my Father. You did not choose me but I chose you. And I appointed you to go and bear fruit, fruit that will last, so that the Father will give you whatever you ask him in my name. I am giving you these commands so that you may love one another (Jn 15:9–17).

This passage indicates quite clearly why Christ can speak of his love for us as "friendship." First, he gives us absolutely selfless, perfect love. He loves us so *selflessly* that he gave his life for us. Secondly, his love for us led him to *share* with us everything he had learned from his Father so that our joy may be complete (cf. Jn 15:11). Thirdly, his divine love *never comes to an end* and the fruits of that love endure forever (cf. Jn 15:16). Even though the apostles did not fully comprehend all that Christ was telling them at that time, he promised to send the Holy Spirit upon them to lead them to complete understanding of the truth and to ultimate union with him in the glory of the Father (cf. Jn 17:24). Christ "emptied himself" (Phil 2:7), coming among us that we might have life in abundance (cf. Jn 10:10) and experience the joy that no one can take from us (cf. Jn 16:22) and the peace that the world cannot give (cf. Jn 14:27). Jesus loves us with perfect, unconditional love. As he said, "I have called you friends" (Jn 15:15).

But the love that Christ offers us far transcends human friendship, just as the love of the Father far transcends the love of a human father for his children. For human friendship is based on the good we discover in each other, which draws and elicits mutual love. Christian charity, instead, is based on faith that God is our Father and that we are all God's children. He has commanded us to love one another as Christ has loved us. St. Paul points out this aspect of divine love: "For while we were still weak, at the right time Christ died for the ungodly. Indeed, rarely will anyone die for a righteous person—though perhaps for a good person someone might actually dare to die. But God proves his love for us in that while we still were sinners Christ died for us" (Rom 5:6–8).

Indeed, Christ died for us when we were still his enemies (cf. Rom 5:10), and he told us to love our enemies and to pray for those who persecute us, if we are to be children of our Father in heaven (cf. Mt 5:43–48). Such love goes far beyond human friendship. Jesus loves saint and sinner. He loves us unconditionally, and he calls us to love others the same way so that our love may be like his.

In addition, Christian charity lasts forever, as St. Paul tells us (cf. 1 Cor 13:8). Whereas friendship cannot begin until one person offers it and another reciprocates, charity always holds out its offer of love, even if rejected seventy times seven times. Jesus asks us to pray for those who reject us and to help them when possible.

Finally, Christ asks that we offer our charity to all, not just a few, with the generosity, kindness, patience, selflessness, and perseverance that St. Paul wrote of: "Love is patient; love is kind; love is not envious or boastful or arrogant or rude. It does not insist on its own way; it is not irritable or resentful; it does not rejoice in wrongdoing, but rejoices in the truth. It bears all things, believes all things, hopes all things, endures all things. Love never ends" (1 Cor 13:4–8).

Because charity far exceeds perfect human friendship, in religious life we strive not merely to be friends but to be *friends in the Lord*, to love as Christ loved us. True charity has all the warmth, tenderness, affection, compassion, and friendliness that Jesus showed to everyone. St. Paul urged: "Welcome one another, therefore, just as Christ has welcomed you, for the glory of God" (Rom 15:7).

The Lord calls every Christian to seek first the kingdom of God and his holiness (cf. Mt 6:33), striving to be perfect as our heavenly Father is perfect (cf. Mt 5:48). Since "God is love" (1 Jn 4:8), we grow in holiness to the degree that we love one another as Christ loved us (cf. Jn 15:12). As religious this is our ultimate goal, our first priority, our primary commitment.

Our religious vows of poverty, chastity, and obedience free us from the obligations of earning money, raising a family, or pursuing an independent career so that we can more freely seek personal holiness and *together form an ideal Christian community*. We will succeed in this task to the extent that we love one another and the people we serve as Christ loved us. God wants us to give witness primarily through our deep and genuine love for one another, more than anything else. "By this everyone will know that you are my disciples, if you have love for one another" (Jn 13:35). In professing our vows, we commit ourselves to live as friends in the Lord.

The Acts of the Apostles shows us a model for religious life: "Now the whole group of those who believed were of one heart and soul, and no one claimed private ownership of any possessions, but everything they owned was held in common" (Acts 4:32). Out of love for God and for each other, they shared everything as friends do. This kind of life demanded much from the first Christians, and Acts tells us how they sustained their community life:

> They devoted themselves to the apostles' teaching and fellowship, to the breaking of bread and the prayers.... All who believed were together and had all things in common; they would sell their possessions and goods and distribute the proceeds to all, as any had need. Day by day, as they spent much time together in the temple, they broke bread at home and ate their food with glad and generous hearts (Acts 2:42, 44–46).

The Church soon discovered that not everyone was meant to live such a communal life, but we have embraced this ideal as our vocation. To continue to live as friends in the Lord today, the nourishment that sustained the first disciples must sustain us too: participation in the Eucharist, the prayerful reading of Scripture, and fidelity to the teachings of the Church. Sharing our insights on these sacred teachings guides us in our communal life and apostolic work. Our commitment to our community will help us make the great personal sacrifices needed to strengthen it. A commitment to live simply will help us to avoid creating artificial needs and making excessive demands on the community. Spending time together enables us to get to know each other and to support one another by our mutual love and affection. Such generosity demands daily common and private prayer and our daily celebration of the Eucharist—the source and symbol of our unity.

Our commitment to live as a Christian community—as friends in the Lord—constantly challenges each one of us to grow in holiness—to love as Christ loved us. In community we do not choose those with whom we live and work. We will grow in holiness by opening ourselves to all others, to welcome those whom we might not find naturally attractive or who annoy us. We have not freed ourselves from the obligation of raising and supporting a family in order to live comfortably and carefree, but so that we can "bear one another's burdens, and in this way...fulfill the law of Christ" (Gal 6:2). In religious life, we primarily seek to be holy as God is holy, and this holiness requires us to renew continually our commitment to love one another as Christ loved us. By emptying our hearts of selfishness, we open them to experience the fullness of life that Christ has promised to all those who follow him as his faithful friends (cf. Jn 10:10).

for Reflection

This is my commandment, that you love one another as I have loved you. No one has greater love than this, to lay down one's life for one's friends. You are my friends if you do what I command you. I do not call you servants any longer, because the servant does not know what the master is doing; but I have called you friends, because I have made known to you everything that I have heard from my Father. You did not choose me but I chose you. And I appointed you to go and bear fruit, fruit that will last, so that the Father will give you whatever you ask him in my name. I am giving you these commands so that you may love one another (Jn 15:12–17).

What does "friendship in the Lord" mean to me?

How would I describe *my* friendship with the Lord? Is it all that I want it to be? In what ways can I nurture the friendship?

How does this friendship influence the way I treat other people?

2

the practice of charity

ONE DAY A LAWYER ASKED JESUS:

"Teacher, which commandment in the law is the greatest?"

He said to him, "'You shall love the Lord your God with all your heart, and with all your soul, and with all your mind.' This is the greatest and first commandment. And a second is like it: 'You shall love your neighbor as yourself.' On these two commandments hang all the law and the prophets" (Mt 22:36–40).

This incident in Our Lord's life contains such a key insight into his teaching that all three synoptics report it. St. John and St. Paul have written many beautiful passages that emphasize the importance of love.

Owe no one anything, except to love one another; for the one who loves another has fulfilled the law. The commandments, "You shall not commit adultery; You shall not murder; You shall not steal; You shall not covet"; and any other commandment, are summed up in this word, "Love your neighbor as yourself." Love does no wrong to a neighbor; therefore, love is the fulfilling of the law (Rom 13:8–10).

St. Paul can say that "love does no wrong to a neighbor" because Christian charity does not seek selfish interests, and sin stems from selfishness. Sometimes out of anger we speak unkindly and critically, wanting to tell someone off and vent our feelings at another's expense. We don't consider the effects our anger may have: the wounded feelings, the angry rebuttals, the bitter arguments, the alienation from our brother or sister in Christ. We don't think of the deep suspicions that will arise because in anger we overstated our case, harshly criticized and unfairly blamed others. In one form or another, all sin flows from selfishness.

But if we really loved our neighbors and sought their good we would not act on angry feelings. If someone wronged us, even deliberately, we would feel more saddened than angered, more sorry that our neighbor had failed God than offended us. We would try to forget the offense immediately without wasting time on self-pity and bitterness. If out of anger we criticize and condemn others for their failings, this shows that we are not very Christian at all, because we haven't even learned to practice the fundamental law of Christ: selfless charity. As St. Paul said, if we sincerely love our neighbors, we cannot wrong them.

Or to take another example, how could we envy another? If we really love God above all else, then we won't set our hearts on intellectual talents, material goods, power, positions and the like. They can help us do good to others but they also bring many cares that can distract us from our first love. If we do not seek these things for ourselves but see them only as a means to serve God (and a dispensable means at that), how can we envy those who possess them? If we envy a fellow priest or community member who has more talents than we do, doesn't this show that we consider our talents as a way to enhance our fortunes? For if we saw talents as a means of serving God better, we would rejoice that another person has them in abundance and uses them to serve God. St. Paul tells us how to regard the different gifts within the Church. "The gifts he gave were that some would be apostles, some prophets, some evangelists, some pastors and teachers, to equip the saints for the work of ministry, for building up the body of Christ" (Eph 4:11–12). A truly Christian charity burns away all envy and personal ambition.

Far from gloating over the mistakes and failures of others, charity sincerely seeks the good of others and the glory of God. The failure of a fellow member of Christ causes sorrow, not rejoicing. A heart on fire with divine charity rejects sin. As St. Paul says: "Love is patient; love is kind; love is not envious or boastful or arrogant or rude. It does not insist on its own way; it is not irritable or resentful; it does not rejoice in wrongdoing, but rejoices in the truth. It bears all things, believes all things, hopes all things, endures all things" (1 Cor 13:4–7).

Charity fulfills the New Law and is the bond of perfection (Col 3:14). Jesus told his disciples, "Just as I have loved you, you also should love one another" (Jn 13:34). His love led him to lay down his life for his friends. For us, laying down our life usually means to give up our ease and comfort when others need us. Christian charity means to do good to one's neighbor, not simply to avoid evil. Christ never said: "*Do not do unto others what you would not have them do unto you.*" We could fulfill that law by living in solitary confinement. Instead, he told us, "*Do to others as you would have them do to you*" (Mt 7:12; Lk 6:31). Fulfilling Christ's law requires practicing all the virtues. Our Lord is quite explicit:

But I say to you that listen, Love your enemies, do good to those who hate you, bless those who curse you, pray for those who abuse you. If anyone strikes you on the cheek, offer the other also; and from anyone who takes away your coat do not withhold even your shirt. Give to everyone who begs from you; and if anyone takes away your goods, do not ask for them again. Do to others as you would have them do to you.

If you love those who love you, what credit is that to you? For even sinners love those who love them. If you do good to those who do good to you, what credit is that to you? For even sinners do the same. If you lend to those from whom you hope to receive, what credit is that to you? Even sinners lend to sinners, to receive as much again. But love your enemies, do good, and lend, expecting nothing in return. Your reward will be great, and you will be children of the Most High; for he is kind to the ungrateful and the wicked. Be merciful, just as your Father is merciful (Lk 6:27–36).

Do we practice charity in our daily lives? How do we treat the person who gets on our nerves, who annoys us by being too emotional or talking too much? How do we act toward the ambitious, boastful, domineering, or disdainful person? How do we react to the self-centered, those who want others to serve them, but who seldom put themselves out for anybody? Honesty requires admitting that we often avoid them. But isn't that really taking as our rule of conduct, "Do not do unto others what you would not have them do unto you"? If we avoid unpleasant persons, how can we help them? What will we do when we have to deal with such people outside the community or rectory? Will we be quick, curt, and unsympathetic, or will we extend compassion to them as did Christ, who died for us? Thinking of this love, St. Paul cried out in astonishment: "For while we were still weak, at the right time Christ died for the ungodly. Indeed, rarely will anyone die for a righteous person—though perhaps for a good person someone might actually dare to die. But God proves his love for us in that while we still were sinners Christ died for us" (Rom 5:6–8).

Selfish and bothersome persons need our compassion, understanding, and love more than others do. Unless in our rectories and religious communities we make a special effort to help those who most annoy us, we will never act like Christians outside the community. For Jesus said that he came to call sinners, not the just. He befriended publicans and sinners. What sinners? Not necessarily robbers and murderers, but petty sinners like ourselves who can make life so hard: the ungrateful, the unkind, the thoughtless, the braggart, the proud, the know-it-all. Jesus asks us not merely to tolerate but to love them because he died for all sinners—including ourselves.

The Gospels tell us how Jesus treated the many annoying persons whom he met. Recall how patiently and firmly he corrected the apostles in their petty rivalry for positions of authority, how calmly he acted when the Samaritans refused hospitality, how warmly he received the women who brought their children to him and the woman who cried after him for a cure. Think of his compassion for the woman at the well and for Zacchaeus, and how Jesus changed their lives by looking deep into their souls to see the goodness they themselves had not recognized. Christ looked beneath the surface, behind the annoying and troublesome behavior to see hearts bereft of self-love and self-respect. He healed them by giving them the love and respect they felt they didn't deserve and hadn't expected.

By enabling them to value themselves and to love themselves, he empowered them to love others.

We can help others most effectively when we love them as Christ loves us—with compassion, understanding, kindness, and patience—especially when they offend us. Christ asks this kind of love from us:

"But I say to you, Love your enemies and pray for those who persecute you, so that you may be children of your Father in heaven; for he makes his sun rise on the evil and on the good, and sends rain on the righteous and on the unrighteous" (Mt 5:44–45).

Difficult persons need us the most, and we need them too. Jesus calls us to practice a love like his—unconditional, selfless, compassionate, and undying. This kind of love opens our hearts to God so he can come and live in us (cf. Jn 14:23) and we can live at peace with him, and with one another.

for Reflection

If I speak in the tongues of mortals and of angels, but do not have love, I am a noisy gong or a clanging cymbal. And if I have prophetic powers, and understand all mysteries and all knowledge, and if I have all faith, so as to remove mountains, but do not have love, I am nothing. If I give away all my possessions, and if I hand over my body so that I may boast, but do not have love, I gain nothing. Love is patient; love is kind;

love is not envious or boastful or arrogant or rude. It does not insist on its own way; it is not irritable or resentful; it does not rejoice in wrongdoing, but rejoices in the truth. It bears all things, believes all things, hopes all things, endures all things. Love never ends. But as for prophecies, they will come to an end; as for tongues, they will cease; as for knowledge, it will come to an end. For we know only in part, and we prophesy only in part; but when the complete comes, the partial will come to an end. When I was a child, I spoke like a child, I thought like a child, I reasoned like a child; when I became an adult, I put an end to childish ways. For now we see in a mirror, dimly, but then we will see face to face. Now I know only in part; then I will know fully, even as I have been fully known. And now faith, hope, and love abide, these three; and the greatest of these is love (1 Cor 13:1–13).

How willing am I to place others' interests ahead of my own?

In what ways might God be calling me to make a greater gift of myself to others?

3

Charity, the Condition for Spiritual Growth

CHRISTIAN CHARITY IS THE BOND OF PERFECTION (COL 3:14).
Our religious communities will be more truly Christian
if love binds us together. Genuine Christlike love is *friendly*.
The more we emphasize this central aspect of community
life, the more our communities will grow.

Many religious begin their apostolic work with great
fervor and enthusiasm, determined to live a life of perfectly
selfless Christian charity. They spend themselves generously for others for several years but then a reaction sets in.
They begin to feel drained, empty, discouraged. All their
labors seem to bear little fruit. Instead of a harvest of wheat,
they reap nothing but weeds. Problems at work and obligations at home burden them. Their community relationships
are polite and reserved, not warm, satisfying personal
friendships. Even God seems to have distanced himself from
them, and they find it difficult to pray. They look back to
days when they felt close to God and found joy in their
lives. Everything looked bright and promising. They wonder where they have failed and perhaps begin to feel guilty.
But the fault may lie in the very structures and conditions of

religious life. These religious may no longer feel joy and enthusiasm not because they have grown lax, but because they are human. For we religious do not always realize that if our human needs go unmet, our spiritual and psychological life suffers. The most basic need everyone has is for love—for genuine, friendly Christian charity—the only "law" the Lord thought we needed.

Recently I visited a college friend of mine who had been an all-American tackle on the Notre Dame football team and who for many years has been a judge in a family court. He also has nine spontaneous, charming, and well-behaved children who deeply impressed me. I was also struck by how gently this big man treated his children. As I was getting ready to leave, I asked him if he had gained any deep insights from his years on the bench. "Yes," the judge replied. "It has taught me to give my children plenty of warmth and affection so that they can grow and mature."

A child cannot grow without genuine love, warmth, and affection. With its profound physical and psychological changes, growth causes stress. Babies must discover how to coordinate their bodies. Children need affection, guidance, and assurance. Teenagers have to cope with academic and social pressures, while feeling volatile and conflicting emotions. They have to mature and to find their places in an adult world. Young people need guidance and protection— much in the beginning, less as they grow older. But they need love at every stage of their growth—not criticism and permissiveness, but a genuine guidance and truly solicitous love.

A too rigid discipline can block avenues of self-discovery and self-expression, possibly leading young people to outright rebellion or prolonged immaturity. Successfully meeting challenges helps us grow in self-confidence and self-esteem. Even if we sometimes fail, we must be allowed to try, learning from our failures and from gentle, kindly advice. Despite setbacks, our self-confidence can grow when others trust and encourage us. The young especially need such emotional and psychological support to grow into responsible adults. But constant criticism and a lack of true affirmation will reinforce their feelings of inadequacy, making it difficult for them to develop the healthy self-confidence and self-esteem they need to confront life's problems successfully.

Those who lack self-esteem often see only their failures and inadequacies, and minimize or overlook their good points. Jesus told us to love our neighbor *as we love ourselves*. So if we do not love ourselves, how can we love our neighbors? Lacking the right kind of self-love, we remain lonely and aloof, unable to give others the love we lack ourselves.

Several years ago, I knew a talented student at the college where I taught. Although quite intelligent and hard working, he often had mishaps. Disasters stalked him. He would stay up all night studying for a test, then fall asleep and wake up when the exam was over. He would drop a test tube in the laboratory, cutting himself badly enough to require medical treatment. Everyone wondered what disaster would strike next.

Toward the end of the year he came to see me. Looking worn and haggard, he seemed a bit disoriented. He told me that all the "accidents" were really deliberate; they were ways he had tried to cry out for help. With his intelligence and other abilities, no one had suspected this.

I called a psychologist friend and arranged an appointment for this young man, who needed immediate help. I called the student's father and soon realized the root of the problem. The father expected great things of his son but did not encourage him or provide emotional support. Terribly afraid to fail, the young man lacked self-confidence and couldn't risk the rejection and criticism he felt sure his failure would entail.

The father wouldn't admit that his son had a problem. The other four children in the family had been quite successful, and this youngest son was the most talented of all. The father didn't come for his son until a week later, after it was too late to meet the therapist's appointment, so the young man didn't get the professional help he needed. He returned to college in the fall but stayed only a few weeks and then left. I have not seen him since and do not know how he fared.

This extreme case illustrates how we can harm others when we love them conditionally. The closer the relationship, the more harm conditional love can do. But when young people are given love and affection, guidance and healthy discipline, then they grow to healthy maturity. When reasonable goals are set, the young know what their elders expect of them, and they can count on the sound advice and emotional support they need. Their determination to prove themselves worthy of the trust others have in them fuels their eagerness to succeed.

As long as we live we continue to grow in one way or another, so we always need unconditional love to grow strong. God will always provide it for us, but we must love each other unconditionally too. Such mutual friendly love helps us more easily bear the burdens of community life, and it also supports us in carrying out our apostolic tasks with vigor and enthusiasm. A religious community or a priests' support group, for example, is a community of friends in the

Lord. Our faith in God allows us to grow into a community of charity, where the friendship which by nature we give only to a few who share our values and interests is given to all those with whom we live and work. Pope John Paul II has said that "love led Christ to the gift of self, even to the supreme sacrifice of the cross. So too, among his disciples, *there can be no true unity without that unconditional mutual love* which demands a readiness to serve others generously, a willingness to welcome them as they are, without 'judging' them (cf. Mt 7:1–2), and an ability to forgive up to 'seventy times seven' (Mt 18:22)" (*Consecrated Life*, n. 42.).

We religious and priests are not always successful in living out the demands of such mutual love called for by our friendship in the Lord. We need grace because our efforts fall short, yet sometimes we come to terms with our weaknesses and settle for simply putting up with one another. We don't help each other overcome our failings and grow in holiness, so we never experience the real joys of Christian living. We may turn outward to our mission for fulfillment and work with great vigor and enthusiasm, but we do not always find the success we had hoped for. If we do not receive from one another the love we need to sustain us in our labors, our inner resources can dry up, leaving our lives empty and joyless. God himself seems distant and prayer grows difficult. We can forget that Christ is present in our midst when two or three are gathered in his name to do his work. We can forget that God manifests himself to each of us through one another, and if we do not work to achieve genuine friendship with our fellow priests or religious, we may lose sight of God's presence among us.

The reason for this lack of warmth in our community and apostolic life falls, in some measure, upon us as individuals. Yet I think some of the reason is also due to our previous training. For generations priests and religious were schooled to discipline their emotions, not to talk about their successes, and to hide their inner frustrations behind a calm and impassive exterior. We weren't allowed to be ourselves; we had to put on Christ—as the superiors imagined him to be. Genuine friendship could hardly develop in such an atmosphere, and if it did, it was suspect. With apostolic frustrations compounded with repression in our community living, no wonder we did not feel the joy of the Holy Spirit. God wants us to experience this joy in our prayer and also in our community life. We may feel dry and empty not because we have grown lax but because our community life is not filling our human needs. We cannot live without human love, for through the love of our friends, God gives us the strength and courage to work with zeal and generosity, and to pray faithfully. Learning to love one another as Christ loved us, to be friends in the Lord, will help us to reap the benefits of Christian living.

It is difficult to understand divine love and to take seriously the demands God's love makes of us. Forgetting that God does not love as we do, with our imperfect love, we impose many conditions on others before we love them. We want them to be kind, gracious, responsive to our moods, faithful, etc. If they fail, we take offense and withdraw our affection. In religious life we can add many more conditions as well, demanding that others observe all the rules, regulations, and customs of our institutes. Although we often criticize others, God does not. He does not love us because we are good but because we are his. His love transforms us. The kindly, merciful acceptance that Christ gave to sinners like Mary Magdalene, the woman at the well, Matthew, Zacchaeus, and Peter drew them from sin to holiness.

In entering a seminary or house of formation, we bring not only our idealism and good will but our imperfections and bad habits too. We all annoy one another at times. When we find others exasperating, we can respond with acceptance, avoidance, or hostility. We put up with one another and behave like strangers rather than friends, brothers, and sisters. We tell ourselves we already have enough burdens to carry. We can easily find excuses when we look for them, but our fundamental commitment to love one another as the Lord loves us directs us to "bear one another's burdens, and in this way...fulfill the law of Christ" (Gal 6:2). Jesus came to help the sinners, the sick, the outcasts, those who did not fit comfortably into society. He sought them out and called them friends.

People are often aggressive, caustic, aloof, or thoughtless because certain events in their lives left them scarred, and they didn't heal properly from these wounds. God understands and shows them mercy. As Christ's followers, we reach out to those who make life difficult, for they most need our love and compassion. We also need them to help us grow in holiness and become more like our heavenly Father. For our generosity, patience, and kindness in dealing with those who annoy us helps us to grow in compassion. When we give others genuine love, they may open their hearts and respond with love. We all profit from mutual benevolence, and so do those we serve in our ministry. For we also bring to our apostolic labors the same sensitivity and compassion developed at home.

By sincerely accepting others and responding to their needs, we create an atmosphere in which everyone can grow. By appreciating and enjoying each other's good qualities, we encourage their development. By forgiving others and treating them with respect and kindness, we foster our mutual growth in the holiness to which our Lord calls us. To the extent that we model our love for others on our Lord's, it can transform them just as his love transformed those he met. Jesus' Spirit in us makes such divine love possible.

God works on earth through his people. When we unconditionally love each other and those we serve, God will draw close to us, our apostolic work will bear fruit, and joy will fill our lives. For we will realize that "wherever charity and love are found, God is dwelling there" (Hymn *Ubi Caritas*). We will no longer feel drained and empty, because his Spirit dwelling in us and among us will indeed become for us a fountain of living water springing up to life everlasting (Jn 4:14).

foR Reflection

We know that we have passed from death to life because we love one another. Whoever does not love abides in death. All who hate a brother or sister are murderers, and you know that murderers do not have eternal life abiding in them. We know love by this, that he laid down his life for us—and we ought to lay down our lives for one another. How does God's love abide in anyone who has the world's goods and sees a brother or sister in need and yet refuses help? Little children, let us love, not in word or speech, but in truth and action (1 Jn 3:14–18).

How do I accept myself? How do I relate to others? Do I accept them or try to control and change them?

In what areas do I need to open myself to God's unconditional love, allowing him to love me so that I in turn can love others?

4

the mystery of the Cross in Our Lives

THE CROSS OVERSHADOWED OUR LORD'S ENTIRE LIFE. HE BECAME a man to save us from our sins through the mystery of his passion and death. As Christians we are baptized into his death and share in his paschal mystery, so that we can also rise with him in glory.

The cross meets us in a thousand forms: in sickness, pain, and fatigue. Everyone experiences anxiety, worry, dread and fear, disappointments and discouragement. Ingratitude, disdain, misunderstanding, and loneliness have intruded into our lives, for suffering has deeply marked our human condition. The cross casts its long shadow over us, but Christ gives us the strength to bear it. For he has told us to take up our cross every day and follow him (cf. Lk 9:23).

But our knowledge of this basic truth often remains purely notional. The mystery of the cross remains difficult to understand. The word "cross" is often reserved for great sufferings, because they leave us no choice but to turn to God. Yet big crosses do not often come into our life; our daily crosses are usually little ones. But big or small they all cause us real suffering, and in the absence of great ones these small ones become our instruments of salvation. Christ tells us to bear these *daily crosses* after him: the inconvenience other people may cause us, difficulties in relationships, burdensome work. These daily, seemingly petty crosses can cause us to fail because we do not see them as the cross Christ wants us to bear, but as nuisances.

It takes faith to see little annoyances as a cross, and we don't always succeed. The apostles themselves did not always succeed either. Recall the Gospel passage when Christ and the apostles were passing through Samaria and were refused lodging (cf. Lk 9:52–56). James and John immediately got angry and wanted to call down fire from heaven to destroy the inhospitable villagers. But Christ restrained them and calmly led them into a neighboring village. They reacted very humanly to a trying situation. They had to learn to carry their daily crosses calmly and patiently after Christ. We can also learn to do this so as to draw spiritual profit from them.

To sanctify our crosses challenges us. It is easy to see our happiness and success as divine blessings and thank God for them, but it is much harder to see life's crosses in this way. A shortsighted view will see only the trial and not divine Providence at work. It is easy to forget that the person who annoys us by boring chatter, or who is always late and keeps us waiting, or who gives us so much trouble is actually a part of God's providence for us. We can easily squander our crosses in impatience, anger or resentment, forgetting that "all things work together for good for those who love God, who are called according to his purpose" (Rom 8:28).

Yet just as rivers form from drops of rain, so small crosses can multiply to become a terrible burden. To work day after day with difficult people or to constantly struggle at prayer can easily weigh us down. But taken a day at a time these small crosses become easier to bear: "Today's trouble is enough for today" (Mt 6:34). Yet in looking back at our lives or into the future, the apparent triviality and futility of life can easily overcome us. With so much to do, we have accomplished so little. Seeing only the problems that lie ahead like sharp stones on an uphill path, we can grow depressed and discouraged. But at moments like these our faith can help us realize that just as the cloud symbolized God's presence among the Israelites in their wanderings through the desert, so he remains with us in the dark and clouded moments of life.

The Israelites' exodus from slavery in Egypt, their passing through the Red Sea, wandering in the desert for forty years, and final entry into the Promised Land hold lessons for our lives as Christians. For through the waters of Baptism Christ has led us from the slavery of sin to freedom. Just as the Jews stayed in the desert for forty years, so we work out our salvation as members of the Church, the People of God, before we enter heaven. The Israelites faced a difficult journey through the parched Sinai peninsula with its searing heat and desert storms. They often lacked food and drink, so that at times the people longed for the flesh pots of Egypt. But God did not forsake them; he sent them manna and quail and gave them water from the rock.

Yet forty years is a long time. The journey from Egypt to Palestine can be made in a short time by foot. Why did God lead them by such a long, hard, circuitous route, on such an apparently useless journey? During those forty long hard years God was forming this bedraggled band of runaway slaves, unlettered and uncultured, into a people peculiarly his own. He was teaching them that as their leader and

king, he would guide and protect them if they were faithful
to him. For this task of founding God's People, forty years of
hardship was not too long. God certainly succeeded well!
Thousands of years later even to today, the Jews, though
dispersed throughout the world, are a people with a sense of
national identity and purpose that has survived untold mas-
sacres and persecutions.

Like the Jews, we too have a special vocation. We are
called to live the Christian life to the fullest in our priestly
and religious vocations, to be a sign within the Church of
total surrender to God. This means witnessing to a complete and absolute dependence upon him in all things both
spiritual and temporal. So God leads us, as he led Moses and
his people, along unfamiliar paths, even bleak and treacher-
ous paths. Suffering can teach us to place our confidence
solely in him, to let him guide, sustain and protect us.
Through the futility and frustration of countless trials, God
works to form us—if we do not resist—into a people peculiarly his own.

Christ also experienced sufferings of all kinds: fickle
crowds, hostility, misunderstanding, fatigue, and his own
apostles' lack of understanding. To all human appearances
he died a failure—his enemies put him to death, Peter
denied him, and the other apostles fled in fear. Only his
mother, John, and a few holy women stayed by the cross to
hear his anguished cry, "My God, my God, why have you
forsaken me?" (Mt 27:46), and his final prayer, "Father, into
your hands I commend my spirit" (Lk 23:46).

Christ lived his whole life in the shadow of the cross,
and as his disciples we must not rebel when crosses come
our way. We may feel weak and far from God; our prayer
may grow so dry and desolate that we feel God has aban-

doned us. But in these desperate moments let us recall the example of our Lord, who traveled the way of suffering before us. We may feel like the disciples on the road to Emmaus—disappointed, discouraged, and saddened at the suffering and death of Christ. They still did not understand the mystery of the cross, which scandalized them even to the point of abandoning Christ. They could not see suffering as a divine blessing, for they still expected that Christ "was the one to redeem Israel" (Lk 24:21). They expected rewards in this life. Jesus appeared to the discouraged disciples, explaining from the Scriptures why it was *necessary* for the Christ to suffer and so enter into his glory (cf. Lk 24:26–27). Jesus' prayer in Gethsemane indicates it was the Father's will that he should suffer and die, but why did Christ have to suffer in order to enter into his glory? The New Testament gives us many reasons.

In taking on our human nature, Christ became like us in all things but sin. He was conceived in his mother's womb and born at Bethlehem, and at Nazareth he grew in wisdom, age, and grace (cf. Lk 2:52). Scripture tells us that Jesus grew through suffering: "It was fitting that God, for whom and through whom all things exist, in bringing many children to glory, should make the pioneer of their salvation *perfect through sufferings…*" (Heb 2:10). Jesus "learned obedience through what he suffered; and having been made perfect, he became the source of eternal salvation for all who obey him" (Heb 5:8–9).

Because pain and suffering are so much a part of our human experience, in sharing our nature Christ "learned obedience through what he suffered" (Heb 5:8). So he shows compassion for us in our human weakness: "For we do not have a high priest who is unable to sympathize with our weaknesses, but we have one who in every respect has been tested as we are, yet without sin" (Heb 4:15).

Early Christian writers used such analogies as redemption, atonement, and reparation to try to make sense of Christ's suffering. Christ said that he "came not to be served but to serve, and to give his life as a ransom for many" (Mt 20:28). Hence just as slaves and prisoners of war could be released by paying a ransom, Christ tells us his death will ransom or redeem us. St. Paul also uses the word "redemption" in reference to the salvation Jesus won for us by his death on the cross (cf. Titus 2:14; cf. 1 Pet 1:18 f.).

But like any analogy, ransom and redemption have their limits. Ransom from whom? Buy back from whom? Furthermore, *how* does the suffering and death of Jesus bring about salvation?

Atonement provides another analogy to probe the mystery. Christ died to atone for our sins. "Therefore he had to become like his brothers and sisters in every respect, so that he might be a merciful and faithful high priest in the service of God, to make a sacrifice of atonement for the sins of the people" (Heb 2:17). And again, "...they are now justified by his grace as a gift, through the redemption that is in Christ Jesus, whom God put forward as a sacrifice of atonement by his blood, effective through faith" (Rom 3:24–25).

But this analogy also has its limits and doesn't explain the mystery of how Jesus' death on the cross saves us. Though we cannot penetrate to the depths of the mystery, we can see that in dying for us, Christ gave us an incontestable proof of his love for us: "No one has greater love than this, to lay down one's life for one's friends" (Jn 15:12). The passion and death of Christ gave proof of his perfect, unconditional, selfless love for us. They also gave proof of the

Father's perfect love for us: "God's love was revealed among us in this way: God sent his only Son into the world so that we might live through him. In this is love, not that we loved God but that he loved us and sent his Son to be the atoning sacrifice for our sins" (1 Jn 4:9–10). Christ offered his life and let his blood run down the altar of the cross to reveal to us that God has always shown us compassion in our sinfulness and our misery. The suffering and death of Christ revealed to us the perfection of divine love.

Knowing the bitterness of his suffering and the depth of his compassion, we can approach him with eagerness and confidence in all our difficulties: "Let us therefore approach the throne of grace with boldness, so that we may receive mercy and find grace to help in time of need" (Heb 4:16).

We need such reassurance, for God does at times seem distant. Think of all the human misery caused by natural disasters: earthquakes, hurricanes, floods, drought, and volcanic eruptions. Thousands of people, many of them innocent children, die horrible deaths. The living can only mourn their dead and face the devastation, knowing that disaster could strike again.

God might indeed seem to be indifferent to our human misery, so he gave us an incontestable proof of his love by sending his own Son to share our lot and to suffer and die for us. "But God proves his love for us in that while we still were sinners Christ died for us" (Rom 5:8). If he could not suffer in his divinity, his Son would become a man and suffer in his humanity, to prove God's love for us.

Furthermore, in Christ we find a way to make our own suffering meaningful. "Those who share in the sufferings of Christ preserve in their own sufferings a very special *particle of the infinite treasure* of the world's redemption, and can share this treasure with others" (Pope John Paul II, *On the Christian Meaning of Human Suffering*, n. 27). By accepting our suffering with perfect trust that God makes all things work together for the good of those who love him (cf. Rom 8:28), we grow in faith, hope, and charity, believing more firmly in God's loving providence for us and making our suffering holy. And that is what "sacrifice" means (from the Latin *sacrum facere*, to make holy). *The essence of sacrifice is faith and love, which make holy the suffering we endure.* Because the crosses we bear make us turn to God more earnestly to find the strength to carry them, our crosses also make us grow in holiness by increasing our faith, hope, and love. By accepting our crosses as Christ did we learn to show greater compassion and more willingly bear one another's burdens. Then we will fulfill more perfectly the law of Christ (cf. Gal 6:2) and love one another as he loved us (cf. Jn 15:12).

Christ's sacrifice was perfect because his love was so great. Because he had such great love for his Father and for us, he wanted to show it even by death on the cross (cf. Phil 2:8). Our love for God will move us to pray, worship, do God's will, and help our neighbor— even at great cost to ourselves.

If love is the heart of sacrifice, what place is there for mortification and penance? We do not practice them as if our sufferings as such please God— not at all. Because we love God, we do penance to regulate our selfish desires and passions. Because we love God, we repair the harm that we and others have done by sinful, selfish actions. Because we love God, we atone for evil by forgiving one another, by asking for forgiveness and by humbly serving the needs of others.

St. Paul said that he made up in his own body "what is lacking in Christ's afflictions" (Col 1:24). To live as friends in the Lord, loving one another with genuine love (cf. Rom 12:9), and to show Christlike love to those we serve in our mission, will offer ample occasion to mortify our selfish inclinations. The practice of charity is the greatest sacrifice. The Lord commands us to live by love, the bond that makes us one in Christ.

for Reflection

For Christ did not send me to baptize but to proclaim the gospel, and not with eloquent wisdom, so that the cross of Christ might not be emptied of its power. For the message about the cross is foolishness to those who are perishing, but to us who are being saved it is the power of God (1 Cor 1:17–18).

I am now rejoicing in my sufferings for your sake, and in my flesh I am completing what is lacking in Christ's afflictions for the sake of his body, that is, the church (Col 1:24).

To some extent we all shrink back from the scandal of the cross. How do I see the cross in my life? What of the small, insignificant "crosses"?

"Everyone who stops beside the suffering of another person, whatever form it may take, is a Good Samaritan. This stopping does not mean curiosity but availability" (Pope John Paul II, *On the Christian Meaning of Human Suffering,* n. 28).

In what ways can I make myself available to others in their suffering?

5

the Call to holiness

*g*ROWTH IN HOLINESS IS QUITE DIFFERENT FROM EFFORTS AT self-perfection. As a work of grace, holiness comes from God, although we need to cooperate with grace. An analysis of various types of skills can illustrate how efforts at self-development differ from the holiness that God gives.

Motor skills, such as athletes develop, consist in the *coordination of movement.* These skills presuppose physical strength and basic natural abilities and require training and practice. For example, the feats that gymnasts perform on the balance beam or the uneven bars demand great talent and long hours of practice. These skills make a good athlete, not a good person. Most people can't do them, and athletes quickly lose these skills unless they constantly practice them. An athlete needs to excel in only one sport. Most athletes specialize in a particular event or play only one position on a team.

We acquire *intellectual habits,* the arts and sciences, when we *order our ideas* and see their proper relationships. Detectives, for example, first gather as many clues as they can find. They then search for a motive that allows them to make sense of all the clues, and solve the crime. Scientists, too, first collect data and then construct a theory to integrate and explain the facts. Understanding comes when all the data fall into place; insight comes from order. Once clearly grasped, these insights remain in the mind and can be shared with others. The intellectual virtues make us good scientists or good mathematicians but not good persons.

Moral habits, the moral virtues, result from our personal commitment to do only what befits a human being. Such a resolve enables us to *order all our voluntary actions* in accord with our human nature. Moral integrity calls for the practice of all the virtues. We cannot be kind if we are not just and patient. But we must make this commitment ourselves; no one else can make it for us. Having made it, we need to be faithful to it in every situation. Time and effort make it easier to do good and avoid evil. Moral virtues, which presuppose a basic commitment to moral integrity, are the most permanent of all habits.

Notice, however, that motor skills and intellectual habits require natural ability. We speak of a "natural athlete" of a "born mathematician" to indicate people with extraordinary talent. But no one is moral by nature; we are moral only by choice. We can freely choose the good and this choice will make us better persons. Hence although not everyone can be an Olympic athlete or a great poet or scientist, anyone can be a good person. For good moral character does not depend on our natural talents but on our free choice. Fidelity to our commitment to moral integrity makes us good persons, not good scientists or sprinters.

But besides the perfection of the athlete, the scientist, the philosopher, and the good person, there is another kind of perfection based on faith, not reason. Since it is based on grace, not human nature, it makes demands on us that go far beyond the demands of morality based on nature. Christ gives us God himself as our standard, our model, our moral ideal: "Be perfect, therefore, as your heavenly Father is perfect" (Mt 5:48). Only faith can grasp this ideal, which only God's grace can bring about. Christian holiness consists in our complete surrender to the will of God our Father. Our task is to remove the selfishness that prevents him from operating in us. Like Mary, we believe that the mighty God will do great things for us if in humility we allow him to work freely in our lives (cf. Lk 1:48–49). The Holy Spirit poured into our hearts inspires, guides, strengthens, and consoles all who open their hearts to him and trust him. The Spirit makes us holy, for Christian holiness is born of faith, supported and sustained by hope, and brought to perfection in charity. The Second Vatican Council stressed that God calls everyone in the Church to holiness: "all the faithful of Christ, of whatever rank or status, are called to the fullness of the Christian life and to the perfection of charity" (*Lumen Gentium*, 40). This call is based on our baptism. Religious consecration deepens and strengthens baptismal consecration and shows forth the Church's holiness in a unique way: "In a very special way this holiness appears in the practice of the counsels, customarily called 'evangelical.' This practice of the counsels, under the impulsion of the Holy Spirit, undertaken by many Christians, either privately or in a Church-approved condition or state of life, gives and must give in the world an outstanding witness and example of this same holiness" (*Lumen Gentium*, 39).

How does this holiness differ from moral perfection, the practice of virtue? Our human nature gives us the basis for judging what is moral or immoral. For example, our social nature makes us depend on society, which requires doing what benefits the common good and avoiding what harms it. This calls for justice and honesty, and respecting the life and property of other people. To take another example, reason can judge that getting drunk is wrong because excessive drinking makes us irrational, which degrades human nature. Moral goodness means acting according to right reason and practicing all the moral virtues. Moral integrity is the basic ingredient of a happy life.

Without denying the moral code based on human nature, Christ has elevated our sights and set a higher standard. He told us to be perfect as our heavenly Father is perfect. Since God is love, we are to love others as God loves us. The life and death of Jesus, the Son of God, revealed God's love for us. Christ's command, "Love one another as I have loved you," sets the standard for Christian holiness. As already noted, Christ loves us in an unconditional, universal, changeless, and absolutely selfless way. This forms the ideal of Christian holiness that we strive after, all the while depending on God's grace.

Comparing the teaching of a moral philosopher like Aristotle with the teaching of Christ brings out very different consequences. For example, Aristotle sees generosity as the virtue that governs spending money—a balance between extravagance and stinginess. Generous persons do not spend more than they make and take only what is justly theirs. They manage their financial affairs prudently so they will have enough money to provide for their needs and to spend on special occasions like a wedding. Generous persons spend the right amount of money on the right occasions and give to the right people for the right reason. Aristotle limits generosity to family and friends and to those who deserve help in their need.

Christ, however, tells us we will find happiness by being poor in spirit, trusting in our heavenly Father to provide for our needs. Just as God takes care of the sparrows and the lilies of the field, he will take care of us too. Jesus told us not to worry about money and material things (cf. Mt 6:19–34). He sent his disciples off on their first mission, with the words: "Take nothing for your journey" (Lk 9:3). He also told them to give generously what they had freely received (cf. Mt 10:8). When the rich young man asked what to do to gain eternal life, Christ told him: "If you wish to be perfect, go, sell your possessions, and give the money to the poor, and you will have treasure in heaven; then come, follow me" (Mt 19:21).

This kind of life inspires those who want to follow Christ in a radical way. Faith in God our heavenly Father enables us to do what reason would never propose. Great saints like Anthony of Egypt and Francis of Assisi have taken Christ at his word, and by their example have inspired thousands to embrace evangelical poverty. During her life, Mother Teresa refused stocks and bonds offered by large corporations for her work for the world's poorest. She preferred to trust only in God to supply the daily needs of her community and her poor. And her community and her works are flourishing all over the world.

To take another example, friendship—especially the friendship of spouses—is the most perfect form of human love. For friends seek each other's good out of selfless love. But most people have only a few close friendships. We do not often find many others to share many interests with, nor in our busy lives do we have the time to spend with others and get to know them in depth.

Christian charity, instead, extends to everyone, for every person is a child of our heavenly Father. Furthermore,

Christ tells us that as children of our heavenly Father, we must love even our enemies and unceasingly offer them our love and forgiveness. For charity never comes to an end (cf. 1 Cor 13:8).

Aristotle spoke of the virtue of friendliness and claimed we should be friendly to everyone. But he said that, unlike friendship, friendliness does not involve emotional ties with those we meet. Christ's command to show compassion, however, implies not only doing good to others but to "love one another deeply from the heart" (1 Pet 1:22).

St. Paul sums up the difference between moral perfection based solely on our own efforts and Christian holiness, boasting "I have suffered the loss of all things…not having a righteousness of my own that comes from the law, but one that comes through faith in Christ, the righteousness from God based on faith" (Phil 3:9).

The pursuit of Christian perfection or holiness builds on moral perfection, the practice of the moral virtues that Aristotle described, for grace builds on nature. Moral virtue requires us to avoid extremes in our desires and actions, for our selfish desires lead us to excesses and defects. Moral virtue curbs our innate selfishness, the root of all sin. Nevertheless, Christian charity transforms our whole moral life by raising our ideal to being children of our heavenly Father. Sharing in the divine nature we are enabled to love with the utter selflessness of divine love.

This kind of holiness does not require us to do extraordinary feats that call attention to ourselves, like an Olympic athlete winning a gold medal. No, Christian holiness usually means doing humble ordinary deeds with extraordinary love. The holy person often goes unnoticed, while athletes or movie stars draw applause and praise for their success.

The Christian community certainly needs talented persons for its apostolic works. To run colleges and universities, for example, requires serious scholars and talented teachers and administrators. Such gifted people naturally rise to positions of prominence and power. They deserve appreciation for their God-given talents and their dedicated efforts to build up the community and the Church.

Great talents, advanced degrees, and positions of power, however, do not ensure holiness and ultimate value in the sight of God. As our Lord warned, "the last will be first and the first last." For God does not reward us for our success but for the sincere love that motivates our actions. How could he do otherwise? For success depends on native talent, which we do not give ourselves, and circumstances we cannot control. Since we have differing abilities and advantages, we cannot achieve the same results. God could not in justice reward us for success. No, he rewards us only for our love, which we give freely and which shows our generosity regardless of how many talents we have. God measures our lives by love, not success.

Love produces fruit that will last. Holy people manifest in their lives the fruits of the Spirit that St. Paul wrote about: "The fruit of the Spirit is love, joy, peace, patience, kindness, generosity, faithfulness, gentleness, and self-control" (Gal 5:22–23). A saint's life, so rich in the fruits of the Holy Spirit, inspires others to imitate it and to seek God as the source of such holiness. This holiness does not come from our natural talents but from the power of God, whose presence in the souls of holy persons shines through their every deed. As Christ said, "Let your light shine before others, so that they may see your good works and give glory to your Father in heaven" (Mt 5:16). God wants only holiness of us. For holiness allows God to work in us so that his will can be done on earth as in heaven, where God's glory shines in all its brilliance and faith gives way to love alone.

for Reflection

I therefore, the prisoner in the Lord, beg you to lead a life worthy of the calling to which you have been called, with all humility and gentleness, with patience, bearing with one another in love, making every effort to maintain the unity of the Spirit in the bond of peace. There is one body and one Spirit, just as you were called to the one hope of your calling, one Lord, one faith, one baptism, one God and Father of all, who is above all and through all and in all. But each of us was given grace according to the measure of Christ's gift (Eph 4:1–7).

How attentive am I to the Holy Spirit who is leading me to holiness?

How do I respond to the call to holiness?

6

holiness and mission

SEVERAL YEARS AGO I CELEBRATED THE FUNERAL MASS OF AN old family friend. He had worked hard all his life and built up a very successful business. He wanted to provide for his large family and assure his children's financial security after his death. But as the business grew it demanded more of his time and energy, leaving less time for his family. His children had every material advantage but not the love and attention they craved. After the burial I went to the family home, and the youngest daughter came up to me and cried, "My father has gone and I never got to know him." I tried to console her. But I knew she was right, for her father had inverted his priorities. At first the business had been his means of providing for his family. Later it became an end in itself, and he sacrificed the real good of his family for the good of the business. If we do not keep our priorities straight we can end up hurting ourselves and others.

This incident reminded me of a poem entitled "The Choice," by the Irish poet William Butler Yeats:

The intellect of man is forced to choose

Perfection of the life, or of the work,

And if it take the second must refuse

A heavenly mansion, raging in the dark.

When all that story's finished, what's the news?

In luck or out the toil has left its mark:

That old perplexity an empty purse,

Or the day's vanity, the night's remorse.

The poet presents us with two options: "perfection of the life or of the work." Choosing to devote our lives to our work may earn us money and fame, but we may lose our souls in the process and never enter a "heavenly mansion." We cannot serve two masters—God and money (cf. Mt 6:24). But keeping our priorities straight can help us balance the various responsibilities that arise from our Christian faith, our religious vows, and our professional work. Then we will be better able to enjoy inner peace and tranquility and avoid constant tension and turmoil.

As Christians our basic commitment is to seek holiness of life. "But strive first for the kingdom of God and his righteousness, and all these things will be given to you as well" (Mt 6:33). Holiness for us Christians consists in loving one another as Christ loved us. How did Christ love us? "No one has greater love than this, to lay down one's life for one's friends. You are my friends if you do what I command you" (Jn 15:13–14). He loves us in a perfectly selfless way. Our love for God and for one another is our primary witness, our apostolic mission. For Christ told us, "By this everyone will know that you are my disciples, if you have love for one another" (Jn 13:35).

By our religious profession we have taken on additional responsibilities. The vows of poverty, chastity, and obedience enable us to live and work together as *an ideal Christian community.*

Our vow of poverty allows us to pool our resources so we can be free of the financial concerns that weigh so heavily on most people. We take this vow not to live in ease and comfort but to be able to serve the needs of others, even when they cannot pay us. By pooling our resources and living simply we can support those in our religious communities who work among the poor at home and abroad. Because of our vow of poverty we contribute to the good of our community, thus depending on each other's support.

By our vow of chastity we surrender the right to have a spouse and children of our own, not to be free of the cares of raising a family but to serve freely all God's children wherever they are: in our colleges, schools, hospitals, and parishes, at home and abroad. Without a spouse and children, our need for close friends who share our values and provide us with affection and camaraderie throws us back on our fellow religious. We need their love, support, and encouragement, and we owe them the same.

Our vow of obedience commits us to work as religious with the approval of our superiors for the good of God's people. It is meant to free us from seeking only our own pursuits so that we can build up the kingdom of God without worrying about advancing our careers. Our vow of obedience calls us to imitate John the Baptist who told his disciples when they complained about Christ's success, "He must increase, but I must decrease" (Jn 3:30). Instead of drawing attention to ourselves, we work humbly and assiduously to bring people to Christ. We can do that best by giving selfless love to others. Support from our community and collaborators helps us to accomplish our goals, for we need each other. Through our vows we commit ourselves to be selfless, open hearted, and gracious in living as religious in a common life.

Our Christian and religious commitments are basic to our apostolic work. But doesn't fidelity to them impinge upon and diminish our apostolic work? Quite the contrary. Our Christian and religious professions help us further our apostolic work by ensuring that it remains truly apostolic. They help us avoid self-centeredness, which could easily spoil the fruits of our labor.

The parable of the sower holds a lesson for us. It has always struck me that "other seeds fell on good soil and brought forth grain, some a hundredfold, some sixty, some thirty" (Mt 13:8). Imagine! Good soil producing 30 and 60 percent! In school, a grade of 30 percent means dismal failure, while 60 percent barely passes. How is it that good people who have accepted the teachings of Christ and become his disciples produce such a meager harvest? It can happen if we are self-serving in our work.

Jesus warns us, his disciples: "Beware of practicing your piety before others in order to be seen by them; for then you have no reward from your Father in heaven" (Mt 6:1). What we do for ourselves is not done for God. Self-centeredness offers a counter witness to the Gospel. The more we center on ourselves, the less we contribute to the kingdom of God. Conversely, the more we practice selfless love and service, the greater our harvest for the kingdom of God. Thus Christ will tell us on the day of judgment: "Inasmuch as you did it to one of these my least brethren, you did it to me." This implies "Insofar as you did it for yourself and not for me you have already received your reward." What we do to build up ourselves does not merit a heavenly reward and spoils our work as Christian apostles.

Sin makes us self-centered, but God's grace makes us selfless. Hence, the more selflessly we love others, the more our actions reveal the selfless love of Christ and draw others to him. As he says: "Unless a grain of wheat falls into the earth and dies, it remains just a single grain; but if it dies, it bears much fruit" (Jn 12:24). Yes, God has given us "this treasure [love of God and the fruits of the Spirit] in clay jars, so that it may be made clear that this extraordinary power belongs to God and does not come from us" (2 Cor 4:7). Those who see how we love one another see Christ living in our midst. As St. Paul puts it, "For while we live, we are always being given up to death for Jesus' sake, so that the life of Jesus may be made visible in our mortal flesh" (2 Cor 4:11).

Although difficult, sorting out all the competing obligations of our complicated lives will help us make selfless love our top priority. Just as our religious life grows out of our basic Christian commitment, so our apostolic work grows out of our religious life, for we have been sent to do our work for the People of God as members of our religious communities. So our work takes on value in light of our Christian and religious commitments. First things first! Fulfilling our religious duties will actually help us to carry on our apostolic work. For an apostle is *sent*, and we are sent to do our work *as* religious priests, brothers, and sisters. We commit ourselves to community living, community prayer, community support, and holiness of life because we have committed ourselves to give our Christian witness *as* members of our religious families. We can witness more powerfully for the Lord when we witness together.

Of course, many reasons can necessitate our doing apostolic work apart from the community, but even then we still follow our religious way of life—strengthened by our vows, our prayer, our dependence on the community for moral and material support. Just as we strive to fulfill our vows, so we are faithful to the daily celebration of the Eucharist, communal and private prayer, to simplicity of life and selfless service, performing our apostolic work in ways that do not oppose but complement our religious life. Remembering that our apostolic work expresses our more basic commitment to serve the needs of others and that the community sends us in obedience will help us to sort out the conflicts and tensions that sometimes arise. Fidelity to our basic commitments will guide us in resolving these problems.

Even if "the work" that the poet speaks about is not our *labor* itself but the *fruits* of our labor, these too can express our faith and love. For "the heavens are telling the glory of God; and the firmament proclaims his handiwork" (Ps 19:1), so we study the world with care and reverence. Then what we say and write will reveal our reverence for God's creation with great insight. The poem, play, or essay we compose will be profound and humane because it will express our insights about our human condition with genuine sympathy. For compassion, which opens our hearts to all people, helps us to understand their plight better. If we choose to seek for the life that Christ wants to give us, we will, within the limits of our talents, strive for excellence in our work as well.

Some might argue that being available to others will make us inefficient, for then the needs of others might hinder us from doing our own work. But would isolation really deepen our insight, enrich our experience, and produce a more excellent work? Rejecting others would no doubt cause more inner turmoil than doing an act of kindness. No, "perfection of the life" enhances and does not hinder "perfection of the work." As the Lord promised, "Strive first for the kingdom of God and his righteousness, and all these things will be given to you as well" (Mt 6:33).

Furthermore, if our commitment to Christ helps rather than hinders our work, so too does our religious profession. For when we do our apostolic work as religious and as priests, we do not have the obligations that most people have. The desire for wealth does not motivate us, for we have given up the right to profit personally from our labors. Any such remuneration belongs to our communities. A desire for fame and recognition does not (or should not) motivate us, for we work as members of our communities, not as independent agents. Instead of trying to win love, affection, and fame for ourselves, we try to lead others to Christ by our genuine love and compassion. The selflessness our religious profession demands of us strengthens our Christian commitment. Both free us to devote ourselves wholeheartedly to our apostolic task, to seek seriously and selflessly "perfection of the work."

Professionalism in apostolic work

Bringing our work up to professional standards may seem at times to conflict with our religious obligations. All of us, no matter what our work, must spend much of our time on mundane matters like attending committee meetings, writing reports, paying bills and raising funds. To work in universities, colleges, high schools, hospitals, or social agencies calls for advanced education. Academics have to prepare lectures and correct student papers, besides doing research and publishing articles and books. Clearly, besides the education we receive as priests, brothers, and sisters, most of us also need additional professional training to serve the people of God in our various institutions. How much does all this have to do with advancing the kingdom of God? How can we balance professionalism with our apostolic mission?

When religious communities owned, operated, and controlled their own schools, colleges, and other institutions, religious could easily think they were doing apostolic work simply by working in them. This assumption was challenged when many communities could no longer maintain their institutions. Religious now often work in institutions they do not own or control. Whether we are a mathematics professor, an administrator, a social worker, or a medical doctor, lay people and nonbelievers can do the same work. Then what makes our work apostolic? Why should we as priests and religious engage in such work? What makes our work truly apostolic and worthy of eternal life?

Our faith in God as our father and Jesus as our brother helps us to see and to love all men and women as our brothers and sisters in the Lord. Our work becomes truly apostolic when motivated by faith, which bears fruit in good works (cf. Jas 2:14–26) and moves us to be compassionate as our Father is compassionate (cf. Lk 6:36). Such faith helps us to purify our motives and avoid self-seeking in serving others. We can make our own the prayer of Mary, the "lowly handmaid" of the Lord, who said: "The Mighty One has done great things for me, and holy is his name" (Lk 1:49).

Such purity of intention and poverty of spirit motivate us to prepare good homilies or lectures, to write thoughtful and scholarly works, to care for the sick and the poor—to do our best at every task. If we receive appreciation and acclaim for our work, we can turn that to the Lord, as he urged us: "Beware of practicing your piety before others in order to be seen by them; for then you have no reward from your Father in heaven" (Mt 6:1). We can thank God for our success and rejoice inasmuch as it can yield more opportunities to serve others and witness to our faith in God.

Tension will always exist between being available to others and caught up in professional work, and we need to feel that tension in our lives. If the trapeze artist does not keep the high wire taut by applying tension from both ends, the wire will sag and the athlete will fall. So too good teachers must have a strong desire both to study and to teach or they will not do their work effectively. But the goal of their study is *"contemplata tradere"*: to delve into and delight in the truth more deeply so as to communicate it more effectively. If we love others as Christ loved us, we will serve them with great love and dedication. The charity of Christ urges us on to do our research, to teach, to counsel, to nurse, etc. with kindness and compassion.

When we try to do our best as professionals and as apostles, we may not have much leisure time, but our Lord didn't have much leisure either. When Jesus found crowds waiting for him, he ministered to them despite his fatigue (cf. Mk 6:30–34). A deep faith helps us find joy in helping others. Our love for those we serve gives us renewed energy; love is like a spring that never runs dry. By making ourselves available to others, we allow them to interrupt us and to disrupt our schedules. We may not accomplish as much as we would like, but at the end of our lives our Lord may put the greatest value on those acts of kindness and Christian charity.

As religious communities we show ourselves as disciples of Christ by the love we have for one another. Christlike

charity—generous, wholehearted, selfless love for one another and for the people we serve—forms the heart of our
community and our personal apostolic work. Such love will
show that our institutions are not only centers of professional excellence, but places where the love of Christ
reaches out to all. Through our various types of apostolic
work, we will take part in the new evangelization that the
Church is calling for today.

Returning to the poem that began this chapter, I would
propose another vision than that of the poet. True "perfection of the life" does not oppose or hinder "perfection of the
work" but rather inspires, protects, and nourishes it. We will
truly bear fruit for the kingdom of God if we can say with St.
Paul: "It is no longer I who live, but it is Christ who lives in
me" (Gal 2:20). By dying to ourselves we produce much
fruit and by loving as Christ loved us, we bear fruit that will
last. For this is how we influence those we serve. We inspire
them to be Christlike, to be perfect as our heavenly Father
is perfect. For us as Christians and as religious, "perfection
of the life" leads to "perfection of the work." For when we
love selflessly, we let God work in us and through us, and he
does everything to perfection.

for Reflection

What then is Apollos? What is Paul? Servants
through whom you came to believe, as the Lord as-
signed to each. I planted, Apollos watered, but God

gave the growth. So neither the one who plants nor the one who waters is anything, but only God who gives the growth. The one who plants and the one who waters have a common purpose, and each will receive wages according to the labor of each. For we are God's servants, working together; you are God's field, God's building (1 Cor 3:5–9).

How is my growth in holiness related to my apostolic work?

What is motivating me to take up an apostolic mission? Who am I working for?

7

Conversion and the Sacrament of Reconciliation

W HY DO WE NEED THE SACRAMENT OF RECONCILIATION? The First Letter of John affirms that we are all sinners who need repentance. "If we say that we have no sin, we deceive ourselves, and the truth is not in us. If we confess our sins, he who is faithful and just will forgive us our sins and cleanse us from all unrighteousness" (1 Jn 1:8–9). To be forgiven, isn't it enough to pour out our sorrow for sin to our compassionate and forgiving Father? Why interpose the priest between God and the penitent, between the sinner and the person offended?

This is what Christ wanted, as the Gospel tells us. Jesus gave Peter the power to bind and to loose (cf. Mt 16:19), and he gave similar powers to the leaders of the Church (cf. Mt 18:17–18). He also bestowed on the apostles the power to forgive sins or to withhold forgiveness, when he breathed on them and said: "Receive the Holy Spirit. If you forgive the sins of any, they are forgiven them; if you retain the sins of any, they are retained" (Jn 20:22–23). Christ did this for a good reason. To understand why we need the sacrament of Reconciliation, it helps to recall what sin does.

Christian holiness consists in loving as selflessly as Christ loved us. But by sin, the opposite of holiness, we refuse to love, refuse to open our hearts to God and to one another. Our refusal to love God disturbs our relationships with others. Sin grows out of selfishness, for by sin we seek our satisfaction at the expense of others. If we lie, cheat, steal, murder, or commit fornication, we exploit or abuse others for our advantage or pleasure. If we ignore the divine commandment to keep holy the Sabbath, refuse to worship God at Mass and excuse ourselves on grounds that we need to rest and relax after working all week, we fail to realize we can find rest by casting our burdens on the Lord. If we habitually put our interests first, we grow indifferent to the prayer of the whole people of God. Like the seed that fell among brambles, our selfish concerns gradually crowd out our love of God and his people.

But those who selfishly desire their gratification and material success more than holiness not only distance themselves from God and his people, they also grow alien- ated from themselves. For material success never lets one rest. We have to protect and preserve our gains, so we can easily become preoccupied with possessions. Pursuing our disordered desires does not free us but ensnares us. Sin and selfishness lead only to self-alienation, not self-fulfillment. This is why Christ tells us to give up our lives (our self- centeredness) and to love as he has loved us in order to find the abundant life of peace and joy he promises us.

By sinning, we alienate ourselves from God, from one another, and from ourselves, and even from the created world by exploiting the environment. We need the sacrament of Reconciliation to overcome our self-imposed alienation.

St. Paul explains how the ideal of Christlike love can help us in this struggle:

> For you were called to freedom, brothers and sisters; only do not use your freedom as an opportunity for self-indulgence, but through love become slaves to one another. For the whole law is summed up in a single commandment, "You shall love your neighbor as yourself." If, however, you bite and devour one another, take care that you are not consumed by one another.
>
> Live by the Spirit, I say, and do not gratify the desires of the flesh. For what the flesh desires is opposed to the Spirit, and what the Spirit desires is opposed to the flesh; for these are opposed to each other, to prevent you from doing what you want. But if you are led by the Spirit, you are not subject to the law. Now the works of the flesh are obvious: fornication, impurity, licentiousness, idolatry, sorcery, enmities, strife, jealousy, anger, quarrels, dissensions, factions, envy, drunkenness, carousing, and things like these. I am warning you, as I warned you before: those who do such things will not inherit the kingdom of God.
>
> By contrast, the fruit of the Spirit is love, joy, peace, patience, kindness, generosity, faithfulness, gentleness, and self-control. There is no law against such things. And those who belong to Christ Jesus have crucified the flesh with its passions and desires. If we live by the Spirit, let us also be guided by the Spirit. Let us not become conceited, competing against one another, envying one another (Gal 5:13–26).

By sinning, we ignore Christ's command of love and so bring disorder and discord into our lives. After sinning, we feel guilty and ashamed, alienated from ourselves.

We may try to overcome our self-alienation by refusing to face our guilt and excusing the evil we have done. But as the Latin proverb says, *"nemo judex suae causae"*—"No one is a judge in his own case." It is easy to overlook our guilt and the evil motives that lurk deep within us. To face ourselves honestly and objectively requires courage. The story of David and Nathan the prophet (2 Sam 11–12) makes clear how we can deceive ourselves about the evil we do. After committing murder and adultery, David apparently felt no guilt. So Nathan the prophet confronted the king and warned him that God would punish him severely for his sin. Confronted with his sinfulness, David admitted his guilt and repented.

This story clarifies the difference between shame and guilt. We feel shame before the gaze of another who knows the evil we have done. We experience guilt, on the other hand, deep within our hearts, even if no one else knows our sin. But we can hide from our guilt, refuse to acknowledge it, block it from our consciousness or excuse it, convincing ourselves that what we did wasn't too bad after all. But when another who knows what we have done looks at us, his gaze penetrates to the center of our being, as Jesus looked at Peter who had denied him (cf. Lk 22:61). That penetrating look strips away our phony excuses and forces us to face ourselves honestly. Our shame dissolves the elaborate defenses we have built up to conceal our guilt. We see our sinful act in light of our moral and religious commitments and are moved to sorrow and repentance, as David was.

By requiring us to confess our sins to a confessor, Christ did not want to humiliate us. He knew we find it difficult to judge ourselves and our motives honestly. We can indeed hide the truth from ourselves, and this could cause us to worry about the sincerity of our repentance. Opening our hearts to a confessor helps us to unburden ourselves and receive the Lord's forgiveness. Because the priest represents

Christ, we can rest assured that we are judged worthy of forgiveness.

Christ never scolded Zacchaeus, the woman at the well, the woman taken in adultery, Peter after his triple denial, or any other repentant sinner. Christ showed such compassion and kindness that sinners dropped their defenses. They saw in his eyes the love and forgiveness that freed them from the burden of guilt they carried. By his kindness, Christ offered them forgiveness and peace. The sacrament of Reconciliation removes the cause of our guilt and reconciles us to God, other people, and ourselves.

First and foremost, the sacrament of Reconciliation reconciles us to God. He loves us even when we sin, but by sinning we close our hearts to his love and act selfishly. But Christ has taught us that the way we treat others is the way we treat him. So to the extent that we close our hearts to our neighbors and enemies, we close our hearts to God. Reconciliation with God requires opening our hearts to our neighbor and repenting of the evil we have done to others and ourselves. The sacrament of Reconciliation restores us to our place in the Mystical Body of Christ. Because we have removed the offense which closed our heart to God's love, God can once more be at home in us and we can be at home with him (cf. Jn 14:23).

The sacrament of Reconciliation also reconciles us to one another and to the Church, the People of God. For by sinning we not only fail to act in a way befitting a child of God, we also fail to maintain the moral level of behavior expected of human beings. We act in a less-than-human fashion. Instead of being honest, kind, and patient, we are dishonest, unkind, and impatient. Our sins inject evil into this world and disrupt the moral harmony that should prevail. What then should we do? When others offend us,

Christ tells us to forgive them even seventy times seven times. When we offend others, he tells us to remove the cause of disharmony and seek their forgiveness. How else can we offer our gift at the altar (cf. Mt 5:23–24)?

When those who have offended us ask pardon, why should we forgive them? Because God pardons all those who ask him for it, and he wants us to love as he loves us. Furthermore, when we forgive we do not let the evil others do infect us. For example, if I had acted viciously toward you and deliberately harmed you, I would expect that when we next met you would lash out at me in anger. If you wanted revenge, then my sin would have poisoned your heart. My reaction to your hostility and hatred might well be, "He deserved it. He had it coming and I'm glad I did it." By holding my sin against me you not only let my failure poison your life, you encourage me to persist in my evil, locking both of us into a hostile relationship. This happens when we fail to forgive.

Suppose instead that I had deliberately harmed you and when we next met you treated me with compassion and kindness, not hostility and hatred. Your virtuous behavior would show me how inhumanly I had acted and I would be more likely to feel shame and sorrow for what I had done. Because you offered me acceptance and love, though I didn't deserve it, I would feel genuine sorrow for what I had done. I would ask your forgiveness and start over, knowing you were still my friend and support. Because you forgave me and refused to let my failings poison your life, you counteracted the poison that had infected my life. Your forgiveness helped me rise again and turn to God, who frees us from our sins.

But what if a person we have offended dies before we ask for forgiveness? What if the evil our selfishness has unleashed has spread far into the community and infected many, like a moral virus? For all sin has social consequences. Selfish attitudes strain our personal and social relationships, making it harder for us to live in peace and harmony. How can we ask forgiveness when we do not know the number or the names of those whom our sin has hurt? What if we repent of our sin and ask forgiveness, yet the person we offended refuses to forgive us? In such situations when we cannot bear the burden of our sinfulness, we turn to Christ, who said: "Come to me, all you that are weary and are carrying heavy burdens, and I will give you rest" (Mt 11:28). When our sister or brother will not forgive us, we turn to the Church, his Mystical Body, to whom Christ gave the power to forgive sin, when he appeared to the apostles after the resurrection and said to them: "Receive the Holy Spirit. If you forgive the sins of any, they are forgiven them; if you retain the sins of any, they are retained" (Jn 20:22–23).

This sacrament also reconciles us with ourselves, for through it God offers us peace. He does not want our sins to burden us. But God cannot forgive our sins until we reject them through sincere repentance. Not even the Church can forgive the unrepentant sinner; sin unrepentantly confessed is retained and the poison remains in the sinner's heart. The confessor must look for signs of true repentance before giving absolution. Hence, Christ tells us (confessor and penitent) "if you retain the sins of any, they are retained."

But when the repentant sinner seeks and obtains forgiveness in the sacrament of Reconciliation, notice what the confessor says over the penitent:

God the Father of mercies

by the death and resurrection of his Son

has reconciled the world to himself

and sent the Holy Spirit among us for the forgiveness of sins.

Through the ministry of the Church

may God give you pardon and peace.

And I absolve you from your sins

in the name of the Father

and of the Son and of the

Holy Spirit.

Because the confessor acts as an ordained minister of the Church, the sacrament of Reconciliation reconciles and restores sinners to the People of God, the Church.

Because the sacrament of Reconciliation so powerfully helps us to grow in holiness, receiving it often benefits us greatly. To confess our sins regularly keeps us honest with ourselves. A regular confessor can look deep into our hearts and see what we may fail to see — not only our potential for evil but our potential for good. He can guide and encourage us besides giving absolution. Absolution from our sins — great or little, mortal or venial — gives us the freedom to move forward.

A person carrying a heavy load has to put it down sometimes and rest. For the load gets heavier and heavier the longer one carries it, or rather, the person carrying it grows weaker. So it happens with our unconfessed sins. The longer we carry them the more they oppress us. We get depressed and bend under their weight.

God wants us to walk through life upright—not with a fearful and heavy heart burdened by guilt and worries. God wants us to live at peace with him, with others and with ourselves. God wants us to experience peace and joy that only Christlike love can provide. Christ calls us to repentance in the sacrament of Reconciliation so that we might enjoy the happiness of a clear conscience and a holy life.

for Reflection

So if anyone is in Christ, there is a new creation: everything old has passed away; see, everything has become new! All this is from God, who reconciled us to himself through Christ, and has given us the ministry of reconciliation; that is, in Christ God was reconciling the world to himself, not counting their trespasses against them, and entrusting the message of reconciliation to us. So we are ambassadors for Christ, since God is making his appeal through us; we entreat you on behalf of Christ, be reconciled to God. For our sake he made him to be sin who knew no sin, so that in him we might become the righteousness of God (2 Cor 5:17–20).

In what area of my life is God calling me to conversion right now?

What steps can I take to live in continual conversion?

8

Blessed are the Poor in Spirit

THE BEATITUDES ARE COROLLARIES OF OUR SINCERE BELIEF that God is our loving Father, who wants only our true good. So we trust him, cast our cares upon him and let him sustain us (cf. 1 Pet 5:7). Faith in God and a sincere desire to do his work free us from the many anxieties and worries that arise from misguided ambition and can so easily wear us out.

The first beatitude is: "Blessed are the poor in spirit, for theirs is the kingdom of heaven" (Mt 5:3). While all Christians are called to be poor in spirit, religious live this beatitude with special intensity. We are "poor in spirit" when we recognize that everything we have is God's gift to us, either directly or through others. Our life, health, talents, education, families, and friends—especially faith and all its blessings—are all gifts. We cannot take credit for any of them. More than we might want to admit, even our successes may result from factors beyond our immediate control. For success comes not only from our hard work and personal dedication, but also from talent, which we do not give ourselves, and from circumstances not of our making, such as the hard work of others. Even our good actions and moral virtues depend on the grace of God, who distributes it as he sees fit. St. Paul challenged us to name something we have that we have not received (cf. 1 Cor 4:7).

In acknowledging that God our Father has freely given us everything we have, we also find reason to trust him to supply all our needs, as Christ has told us to do. This frees us from anxiety, like children who trust their parents will take care of them. If we "strive first for the kingdom of God and his righteousness" (Mt 6:33), we will try to distinguish clearly between our needs and wants, and between those wants that benefit us and those that harm us. On the one hand, we want pleasurable and useful things that help us to live happy and fruitful lives, like nourishing food and tools to do our work. On the other hand, we can want what is enjoyable but bad for us, like junk food, or we can do things that profit us but are immoral, like stealing, or that are pleasurable but immoral, like fornication. We can also seek pleasures that are moral when used in moderation, but which become bad when indulged in excessively, like eating or exercising too much. Even useful things can be desired in excess so that they clutter up our lives and hinder us from seeing what truly matters. God asks us to seek *first* the kingdom of God and his holiness, trusting him to supply our needs, so as to better see what is truly good. Although it takes a lifetime of growth in insight and freedom, God will help us to gradually free ourselves from the excesses and clutter that can so easily fill our lives.

In this way we can witness to the Gospel ideal of a poor and simple life even in the midst of the consumerism and materialism of our culture, as Pope John Paul II reminds us: "*Another challenge* today is that of a *materialism which craves possessions*, heedless of the needs and sufferings of the weakest, and lacking any concern for the balance of natural resources. The *reply* of the consecrated life is found in the profession of *evangelical poverty*" (*On Consecrated Life*, n. 89).

This poverty leads us to entrust our lives to God and seek first his kingdom and his holiness. It teaches us to appreciate and value what we have. As poor in spirit we are grateful to God not just for food and clothing, but for everything. We recognize the beauty of the world as God's gift. God gives us all the beauties of nature: the wildflowers and the song of birds in spring, the cool breezes and the refreshing rains of summer, the brilliant foliage and the early morning frosts of fall, the fresh white snow and the crystal ice that covers ponds and lakes in winter.

Artists enrich our lives with the beauty of their music, painting, sculpture, and architecture. The beauty of mind and heart that we discover in family, friends, and good people everywhere evokes our gratitude and incites our admiration. Our faith tells us that God has given us all these gifts as signs of his love. God wants us not only to appreciate but to *treasure* them as *his* gifts, never to be taken for granted.

While rich persons can also be poor in spirit, wealth can easily tempt us to self-sufficiency. In the Gospel Jesus clearly warned us of the danger of riches. Luke's parable of the rich fool ends with a stern warning (cf. Lk 12:16–21). St. Paul also showed great concern for the poor, taking up collections for their needs. If we have faith and are poor in spirit, whether we ourselves are rich or poor, we see that those who suffer want are also God's gifts to us. They elicit our self-sacrificing love when we act as God's instruments in meeting their need. To them we can give without hope of return except from the Lord, who considers as done to himself what we do for the least of his brethren. And for sharing God's gifts to us with those who need them, God gives us eternal life. As poor in spirit we identify with the poor and serve them gladly. "This witness will of course be accompanied by *a preferential love for the poor* and will be shown especially by sharing the conditions of life of the most neglected. There are many communities which live and work among the poor and the marginalized; they embrace their conditions of life and share in their sufferings, problems and perils" (*On Consecrated Life,* n. 90).

As poor in spirit we generously give to others, knowing that our heavenly Father takes care of us. If we are to give freely to those in need, however (cf. Mt 10:8), we carefully manage our goods and live a simple life so as to have something to give away. Simplicity helps us keep our heart focused on God, so that we will not clutter our lives with unnecessary possessions that can distract us from our primary goal: holiness, or loving as Christ loves us. "If riches increase, do not set your heart on them" (Ps 62:10).

Poverty of spirit helps us to avoid becoming preoccupied with ourselves, nor overly concerned about our success and failure. Of course it delights us to help others, but we don't want to take credit for ourselves. Poverty of spirit helps us recognize that we can only do good through God's grace and rejoice in it, striving to remove from our lives the sin and selfishness that can obstruct the action of grace. As a clean window lets sunlight into the room, so we try to let God's light shine through us, without trying to take credit for the good that occurs in the lives of those we serve. As poor in spirit, we happily acknowledge that we are "unprofitable servants," as Christ told us to do (cf. Lk 17:10).

Our Lord warned the apostles: "I sent you to reap that for which you did not labor. Others have labored, and you have entered into their labor" (Jn 4:38). The good we may want to claim credit for may have been done chiefly through the work of others. We don't know how the Lord views success, so we let him judge our success and failure without being puffed up by the one or downcast by the other. St. Paul tells us that God will reward us *not* for our success but for our labors (cf. 1 Cor 3:8). Poverty of spirit motivates us to work at our tasks for love of God and neighbor, to do the best we can and leave the rest to God.

Poverty of spirit also helps us not to be concerned about making a name for ourselves, for we want to bring others closer to the Lord, not to ourselves. John the Baptist exemplified this when he told his disciples, who had seen the crowds flocking to Jesus, "He must increase, but I must decrease" (Jn 3:30). St. Paul also reminds us:

> What then is Apollos? What is Paul? Servants through whom you came to believe, as the Lord assigned to each. I planted, Apollos watered, but God gave the growth. So neither the one who plants nor the one who waters is anything, but only God who gives the growth. The one who plants and the one who waters have a common purpose, and each will receive wages according to the labor of each. For we are God's servants, working together; you are God's field, God's building (1 Cor 3:5–9).

If self-love and a spirit of self-importance motivates us, we become "a noisy gong or a clanging cymbal" (1 Cor 13:1). But poverty of spirit can motivate us to preach the word without any show of oratory or worldly wisdom (cf. 1 Cor 2:1) that could obscure Christ's message. If our preaching, teaching, or counseling gains results, we will thank God for the good done. For he has promised to send the Holy Spirit to lead us to the complete truth (cf. Jn 16:13), to help us speak from the abundance of our hearts (cf. Mt 12:34), and to give us the eloquence and wisdom that our adversaries cannot resist or contradict (cf. Lk 21:14–15).

Because it helps us develop a more spiritual outlook, poverty of spirit helps us to embrace our pain and suffering as a means of purification and as an occasion to grow in faith and trust in God. Like St. Paul, who said "I can do all things through him who strengthens me" (Phil 4:13), poverty of spirit helps us to realize our weakness and to face difficulties with confidence not based on our strength but on God's power working through us.

As poor in spirit, however, we accept full responsibility for our sinfulness. For in sinning we refuse to let God work in us, act selfishly, and seek our immediate satisfaction to the exclusion of God and neighbor. As poor in spirit we face our sins honestly and repent sincerely. But we never grow despondent, knowing that God forgives us and only asks that we forgive those who offend us. God makes all things—even sin—work together for the good of those who love him (Rom 8:28). We are content to let the Holy Spirit lead us in prayer (Rom 5:26–27). Conscious that all good things come to us from our heavenly Father, we take to heart St. Paul's advice: "Give thanks in all circumstances; for this is the will of God in Christ Jesus for you" (1 Thess 5:17–18).

When our Lord sent the apostles on their first mission, he gave them explicit instructions that clearly show the importance of poverty of spirit (cf. Mt 10:5 f.). He told them to seek out "the lost sheep of the house of Israel" and "to cure the sick, raise the dead, cleanse the lepers, cast out demons," while proclaiming that the kingdom of heaven had come close. Jesus instructed his disciples to minister to those who could make no return, to the poor, to the outcasts of society. He told them to give freely what had freely been given to them. They were to make *no* provisions for themselves: no money, no traveling bag, no spare tunic or shoes, no staff. Although those specific instructions were for that time and needn't be followed literally today, Jesus wanted them—and us—to witness to the message by simplicity of life. He even told them not to worry about defending themselves against opponents, for God would speak in them. Their poverty would give a witness no one could contradict. But the Lord told them not to expect success, for they were not above their Master. They were to go and witness to their faith and trust in God, the Father of all, and offer God's peace to everyone. Even if others rejected that peace, it would come back to them.

"Peace," St. Augustine tells us, "is the tranquility of order." When we can rejoice because we completely depend on God, our loving and compassionate Father, then we stand in the right relationship to God. We will experience the peace that the world cannot give (cf. Jn 14:27) and the joy that no one can take from us (cf. Jn 16:22). The kingdom of heaven truly belongs to the poor in spirit.

foR Reflection

> *There is great gain in godliness combined with contentment; for we brought nothing into the world, so that we can take nothing out of it; but if we have food and clothing, we will be content with these. But those who*

want to be rich fall into temptation and are trapped by many senseless and harmful desires that plunge people into ruin and destruction. For the love of money is a root of all kinds of evil, and in their eagerness to be rich some have wandered away from the faith and pierced themselves with many pains (1 Tim 6:6–10).

Do I trust in God more than possessions? Is God asking me to let go of something I don't really need?

How does a life of evangelical poverty speak to a culture immersed in materialism?

9

the Vow of poverty

IN THE 1960s PRESIDENT LYNDON JOHNSON DECLARED A WAR on poverty. He wanted to use the federal government's resources to help poor Americans to support their families, get a good education and a decent job, thus giving the destitute hope for a better life. It was a grand scheme and much remains to be done to achieve that ideal. As members of the Church we can make common cause with such noble efforts to foster social justice and eliminate grinding poverty.

The vow of poverty does not mean destitution, which is not desirable for anyone, and we do not embrace it in religious life. We religious are not factually poor and do not live as the poor do. Our religious communities provide all our necessities: food, shelter, health care, education, companions who care about us. We actually live quite well. We have beautiful, peaceful places of prayer, and community residences that provide privacy, comfort, and areas where we can gather to enjoy each other's company. We have times of rest and relaxation and prayerful liturgical celebrations that lift up our hearts and bond us together as members of the same religious family. We have the best education available and institutions that allow us to influence the lives of others. God has certainly given us the hundredfold that Christ promised to those who leave everything to follow him (cf. Mt 19:29).

All this is as it should be. For active apostolic communities need resources to support their apostolic works, educate their members, care for their elderly and sick, and support those laboring among the poor and the dispossessed. They need to provide properly educated and trained personnel to maintain a strong Catholic presence in their institutions and to support worthy projects fostering justice and peace.

All this throws light on the purpose of the vow of poverty. By this vow we commit ourselves to pool our resources, to give our earnings to our religious communities, and to live a common life. Even if we retain ownership of private wealth, we commit ourselves never to profit from it personally and to live only on community funds, as the first Christian community did (cf. Acts 2:44–45).

Why do all this? To free ourselves from the burdens that go with acquiring and accumulating wealth so that we can wholeheartedly pursue our Christian ideal—the love of God and the service of our neighbor. "Evangelical poverty forcefully challenges the idolatry of money, making a prophetic appeal as it were to society, which in so many parts of the developed world risks losing the sense of proportion and the very meaning of things" (*On Consecrated Life*, n. 90).

Always keeping in mind the purpose of our vow of poverty will help us live it well. Otherwise, free from financial concerns, we could act irresponsibly and selfishly, giving a scandalous counter witness to our religious profession, drifting into a style of life that belies our religious commitment. Thinking we are entitled to live like other people who do the kind of professional work we do, we could become materialistic, expecting to have the vacations, travel allowances, recreations, and expensive clothes that they have. We might prefer the lifestyle of the professional and the well-to-do. That would leave us little in common with the poor who must struggle to make ends meet, to raise their children, and to provide for their education. They cannot move in the privileged world of the professional and the wealthy.

Besides that, we might begin to notice where other members of our communities go on vacation, their travels, cars, clothes, etc., perhaps feeling envious and thinking that we deserve similar things. Or we can resent those whose positions require them to travel or to attend fund-raising events and mingle with the wealthy. To allow such sentiments to invade our hearts makes void the purpose of our vow of poverty.

St. John warns us against pride in possessions (cf. 1 Jn 2:15–16). We vow to give up the pursuit of personal wealth and to pool our resources, living a common life in order to free ourselves to love God and serve our neighbor. If we keep that purpose clearly in mind, we can use our freedom from financial responsibility to dedicate ourselves to the needs of those we serve, caring more about their service than about our ease and comfort. We will not envy the material advantages that others enjoy. Convinced that God blesses the poor in spirit, we will want to keep our lives simple, uncomplicated, and free from needless clutter. Our vow of poverty will lead us to this.

For we exercise an apostolic presence not so much by the work we do but by the selfless Christlike love that emanates from our hearts. Atheists can do our work but they do not intend to witness to the love of God. Christ rejected the temptation to spread the kingdom of God by aligning himself with the kingdoms of the earth, with the rich and powerful. Following his example, we will not let wealth seduce us or desire the power we could wield when aligned with the powerful and influential. No, we rely on the power of God and enjoy those blessings that can satisfy us much more than the pleasures this world can offer. We experience the love, joy, and peace that this world cannot give or take away. To the extent that we root our lives in love, we will not let the allure of wealth and the pleasure it can buy deceive us.

Jesus told us: "I came that they may have life, and have it abundantly" (Jn 10:10). He also said "those who lose their life for my sake will find it" (Mt 16:24). What does he mean?

The Lord is telling us not to pursue selfish pleasures that will make us insensitive to the needs of others. For we do not find ourselves in pleasure; we lose ourselves in it. Think of how quickly time passes when we enjoy ourselves. We can forget the burdens of the day when we play soccer or tennis or take a walk or pray. Putting aside the pressures of our lives for a while, we can relax so that we can bear our burdens again. Recreation refreshes us precisely because we can forget our burdens and lose ourselves in our pleasurable activities. The pursuit of pleasure, consequently, does not put us in touch with ourselves. While good in moderation, pleasure pursued as our main goal in life alienates us from ourselves. Self-indulgence does not bring self-fulfillment. Our Lord asks us to give up a life of pleasure so that we might enjoy a spiritually rich and abundant life.

Christ provides us with a rich and abundant life because he gives meaning and purpose to everything we do. Without purpose, we feel bored or hopeless and complain, "What kind of life is this?" Christ provides ultimate meaning and eternal significance by his revelation of God the Father. Our Christian faith makes everything meaningful, for we believe that "all things work together for good for those who love God, who are called according to his purpose" (Rom 8:28). We have a clear vision of life's purpose: "Be perfect, therefore, as your heavenly Father is perfect" (Mt 5:48), and "love one another as I have loved you" (Jn 15:12). In selfless love we find our greatest joy, as every friend or parent knows on a human, limited scale. We find true fulfillment or happiness by loving others and making a sincere gift of ourselves.

Our vow of poverty safeguards us from "the desire of the eyes, the pride in riches" (1 Jn 2:16) that can deceive us into thinking that we will find fulfillment by filling our lives with more and more things. Wealth can buy pleasure, but not happiness. Happiness comes from being in touch with oneself and at peace with God. "If anyone loves me he will keep my word and my Father will love him and we will make our home in him" (Jn 14:23). We find happiness when we are "at home" with God in the depth of our souls where he is "at home" in us.

The vow of poverty holds great importance for us, keeping us centered on the pursuit of holiness. It helps us avoid cluttering our lives with things that can give us pleasure but not joy, peace, and happiness. Our vow of poverty helps us to practice poverty of spirit and so find happiness as individuals and as a community. Free of unnecessary things, we can concentrate on the essentials in our lives and give witness to the world of our Christlike love for one another and for those we serve.

This witness includes respect for the earth's resources, safeguarding them for future generations. As Pope John Paul II has said, "The call of evangelical poverty is being felt also among those who are aware of the scarcity of the planet's resources and who invoke respect for and the conservation of creation by reducing consumption, by living more simply and by placing a necessary brake on their own desires" (*On Consecrated Life,* n. 90).

This attitude will help us to regulate our use of resources. In serving others, we certainly need the means necessary to work efficiently and well. Modern machines such as computers can save us much time. But if we have these wonderful technological marvels, the spirit of poverty will help us to use them responsibly. The time they save can be used for purposeful work. If we squander the leisure time that inventions have made possible, we are hardly profiting from them. Besides this, we can become addicted to our machines and spend our time glued to our computer and modem. We might surf the Internet as an endlessly amusing pastime, and for lack of discipline and true purpose, waste our time. It takes discernment to use technology wisely, making sure it does not take over our lives.

Prayer, contemplation, and spiritual reading help us develop our union with God and enjoy fullness of life. Loving one another and the people we serve expands our hearts. Spending time and bonding with the persons we live and work with may mean getting away from our machines, televisions, and computers to experience directly the world around us with its sights, sounds, and scents. We can use our computers to escape the burdens of human interaction, especially if we are shy or uneasy in social relationships. The world may not be neat and tidy and at times can intrude into our lives more than we might like, but the controlled and detached information coming from our computer screen gives us only a limited experience of it. Human and spiritual growth calls for developing not only our minds, but all the dimensions of our personalities. Computers can offer many opportunities to grow in knowledge and efficiency. But they can also pose a threat to our personal development, to community life, and to our apostolic work if we use them to withdraw from essential human relationships and waste our time in the endless pursuit of computer entertainment. If our vow of poverty makes the latest technology available to us, the spirit of poverty will assure us of using it well.

ƒor Reflection

The one who sows sparingly will also reap sparingly, and the one who sows bountifully will also reap bountifully. Each of you must give as you have made up your mind, not reluctantly or under compulsion, for God loves a cheerful giver. And God is able to provide you with every blessing in abundance, so that by always having enough of everything, you may share abundantly in every good work. As it is written, "He scatters abroad, he gives to the poor; his righteousness endures forever." He who supplies seed to the sower and bread for food will supply and multiply your seed for sowing and increase the harvest of your righteousness. You will be enriched in every way for your great generosity, which will produce thanksgiving to God through us (2 Cor 9:6–11).

How does a life of hard work express the evangelical spirit of poverty?

Are my needs simple (few), or do I find myself wanting more and more things in order to be happy? How can I set my heart more fully on God?

Celibate Chastity for the kingdom of god

The Gospels contain very few references by our Lord to the virtue of chastity. Even when dealing with those who had sinned against chastity, he forgave them and said only, "Go your way, and from now on do not sin again" (cf. Jn 8:1–11). Considering the importance Christian asceticism gives to the virtue of chastity, our Lord has said surprisingly little indeed. Yet he did not need to say more. Celibate chastity "for the sake of the kingdom of heaven" (Mt 19:12) is an expression of love for God and neighbor.

When asked which commandment is the greatest, Christ told us that we are to love God with our whole heart, soul, mind, and strength, and to love our neighbor as ourselves (cf. Mt 22:34–40). Jesus makes love of God and neighbor *inseparable*. He even tells us to show mercy to one another as God shows mercy to us, and that God counts as done to himself whatever we do to others. By truly opening our hearts to God's love, we will open them to everyone, even those who wish us ill. But to close our hearts to our neighbor is to close them to God. This is why Christ commanded us to love one another as he loved us and spoke of us as his friends. Belief in God as our Father calls us to love everyone as our brothers and sisters.

Love forms the basis of Christian life, and most people live this out especially in marriage. Christ showed his esteem for marriage by celebrating with his mother and disciples at the wedding feast of Cana, by forbidding divorce and remarriage, and by welcoming and blessing children, the fruit of marriage. The love of husband and wife, St. Paul would later teach, symbolizes the love of Christ and the Church (cf. Eph 5:21–33). For as husband and wife become one flesh in marriage, we are joined to Christ and to one another in his Mystical Body. Marriage is a sacrament, which the married couple confer upon each other in the presence of the priest, the Church's witness. Marriage is a holy state of life that originates in Christian love, is supported by the abiding presence of the Holy Spirit and is lived as an expression of Christ's selfless love for us.

Yet Christ also spoke approvingly of another state of life — celibate chastity for the sake of the kingdom of God. He did not propose this state of life for everybody but for those who can accept it (cf. Mt 19:11–12). Celibate chastity is a special vocation within the Church, within the Mystical Body of Christ. Just as married couples share their love with one another, their children, their neighbors, and the whole Church, those called to celibate chastity for the sake of God's kingdom witness to the love of God in a special way — a way which has extraordinary value in God's eyes. He called his own mother, the ever-Virgin Mary, to this kind of life.

How is celibate chastity for the kingdom a special gift of God? By a vow of celibate chastity, a person expresses total dedication to God and neighbor even to foregoing the intimate love, companionship, and support of a spouse, and the joy of having children. A vow of celibate chastity for the sake of the kingdom of God reveals a profound commitment to seek first the kingdom of God and his holiness, to love selflessly as Christ told us to do, and to leave one's heart completely free to love God and to serve God's people, our brothers and sisters in Christ. It is a charismatic sign of the kingdom of heaven, an eschatological sign that points to eternal life.

Experiencing the love that God pours into our hearts can affect us so profoundly that other loves pale before it. Celibates can experience so strong a desire for intimacy with God that it makes them willing to forego the special intimacy of married life. For marriage demands of spouses a union of mind, heart, and body that the celibate wants to reserve for God alone. Giving up the joys and obligations of a family leaves the celibate free to serve all God's people.

St. Paul expresses this contrast clearly when he writes:

> I want you to be free from anxieties. The unmarried man is anxious about the affairs of the Lord, how to please the Lord; but the married man is anxious about the affairs of the world, how to please his wife, and his interests are divided. And the unmarried woman and the virgin are anxious about the affairs of the Lord, so that they may be holy in body and spirit; but the married woman is anxious about the affairs of the world, how to please her husband. I say this for your own benefit, not to put any restraint upon you, but to promote good order and unhindered devotion to the Lord (1 Cor 7:32–35).

St. Paul emphasizes that celibates devote themselves totally to the work of the Lord. But to be a celibate for the kingdom of God, though noble, is indeed hard. For sex, so basic to our being, is powerful, natural, and good. Sex is a basic drive that comes with all life. Sex is powerful, for it shapes our personalities in the various stages of our development, and to regulate it calls for great maturity and virtue. Sex is natural and good because it is God-given and can generate tremendous energy, vitality, and warmth, which we need in order to be truly human, true men and women of God. While having a great respect for the power that sex can have over us, we need not fear it if we are faithful to God. If our hearts remain fixed on him then the fire of charity will consume the embers of sexual passion. We can then channel all the energies of our sexual nature into prayer and labor for the People of God. By harnessing our sexual energies to feed the flames of our zeal, we will be able to live a chaste life faithfully.

As the physical counterpart to love, sexuality has the limitations of the physical. It requires a commitment to spouse and children. To be free to open our hearts to everyone, religious and priests vow to live heroic lives of celibate chastity. Our vow of chastity enables us to dedicate ourselves entirely to the love of God and the selfless service of God's people. Chastity offers a way of making a total gift of self. As Pope John Paul II has said, "Those who in life choose continence for the kingdom of heaven do so…in view of the particular value connected with this choice and which must be discovered and welcomed personally as one's own vocation" (General audience, March 10, 1982).

Keeping this ideal in mind helps us live this vocation with generosity and love and avoid the pitfalls of selfishness. For we need to consider another less noble aspect: a vow of chastity also frees us to devote more time to ourselves. Married people have to make profound adjustments in their lives: they need to consider their spouses and children, the likes and dislikes, moods, weaknesses, and needs of each member of the family. Perhaps spouses cannot devote as much time to religious matters as celibates do, but good spouses and parents certainly cannot devote much time to themselves. Family affairs occupy them constantly day and night.

Religious, however, have no such immediate and pressing family responsibilities. Our God is a hidden God and, unlike a wife or husband, he speaks to us so softly that we can easily turn a deaf ear. To the degree that we ignore God we will ignore God's children and make a god of ourselves. If our vow of chastity becomes divorced from Christian charity and loving service, then chastity becomes either a sacrifice unfairly imposed and bitterly resented, or the price paid for freedom from family obligations. Without a spouse we enjoy peace, quiet, and independence, but we can end up by keeping aloof and distant from the people God calls us to serve. We might make ourselves unavailable to them and see every call as an interruption. Instead of welcoming people we can become testy and curt with visitors.

As Christian celibates, we cannot separate chastity from charity, otherwise we will become ensnared by selfishness. Our celibate chastity is meant to provide the ideal condition for a life of prayer and loving service to the People of God.

Priests and religious who divorce celibate chastity from charity might never realize how selfish they really are; for in the past, spiritual writers taught us to remain aloof and detached from people. Chastity was considered such a rare and delicate blossom in a seamy, sordid world that it had to be protected by an array of Victorian proprieties. Religious were expected to be dignified, distant, and detached, calm and serious, kindly but certainly never friendly, mindful of their sublime state.

These writers, of course, were not wholly wrong, but they were far from right. Certainly celibate chastity must be protected, but this does not mean stoically suppressing our feelings and emotions. Chastity calls for a certain detachment, but this is something positive. It means being detached from bodily pleasures but deeply attached to the joys of the soul, taking a God's-eye view of earthly things. God looked down on his creation and said it was good, indeed very good, and so we recognize the beauty of this world. Yet God does not want us to set our hearts only on creatures, but to use them to raise our hearts to God, as did the psalmist: "The heavens are telling the glory of God; and the firmament proclaims his handiwork" (Ps 19:1). Chastity cannot be cold, frigid, and aloof, for nothing can grow in cold storage, and a virtue either grows or dies.

The Gospel shows us Christ feeling moved over people's sorrows. He cared about the people around him and made himself approachable. The Savior had compassion on the multitudes, wept over Jerusalem, looked on the rich young man and loved him, and was deeply moved by the generosity of the widow putting her mite into the treasury. Christ cherished Peter and John as special friends. The grief of his friends Martha and Mary brought him to tears, and he brought their brother Lazarus back to life. We see in the Scriptures a Son of Man who so enthralled the crowds that they would walk into the wilderness to hear him and even forget about eating. He placed his hands gently upon the sick to cure them and blessed the children brought to him. Jesus was not distant and aloof. With warmth and compassion he reached out to people, and he invites us as his disciples to do the same.

Celibate chastity is the ideal condition for reaching out to others with Christian charity, for charity alone sustains and gives value to celibacy. Charity also gives it warmth and fruitfulness. Without charity, celibacy is sterile, cold, and forbidding. In an impersonal age of machines and computers, of identification cards and social security numbers, people want desperately to be known and loved as individuals. Real people resist being processed and programmed. We Christians cannot do the work of God if we remain cold, aloof, and distant from one another. Priests and religious are called to be a father and mother, brother and sister and friend. This calls for warmth and understanding, tenderness and compassion. Chastity requires us to be available and approachable, willing to spend ourselves for all. Today, perhaps more than at any other time in Church history, priests and religious need to imitate Christ who had compassion on the multitudes.

Is there any danger to our chastity in all this? Yes, of course. People are lovable and human love has its sexual components. But let's not exaggerate the dangers. Aloofness poses a far greater danger to chastity than involvement. Staying aloof and distant out of fear can breed loneliness, and it is not good to be alone. We cannot suppress the power and vitality of our nature, and if we try to do so by keeping aloof from others, then its energies will erupt and cause havoc within ourselves. No, we cannot be Stoics or Jansenists. We are to be fully human because our nature comes from God, and his grace perfects and strengthens nature.

Still, to love deeply without passion is difficult. The English language itself gives eloquent testimony to the struggle chastity requires. Consider the words cognate to chastity: "chasten," "chastise," "castigate"—all of them imply bodily discipline. Human experience witnesses to St. Paul's policy: "I punish my body and enslave it, so that after proclaiming to others I myself should not be disqualified" (1 Cor 9:27). Chastity calls for self-discipline, but by seeing our chastity in the light of Christian charity, our effort will grow out of love.

Of course temptations will come, but how else can virtue grow? God is always faithful. We can trust him, for he is our help and our shield. "For God did not call us to impurity but in holiness" (1 Thess 4:7). The celibate chastity of the priest and religious is a noble ideal, a ringing challenge to a sex-crazed society. It shows our total commitment to Christ and our fellow human beings. Difficult? Of course it is! But Christ has told us, "Take courage; I have conquered the world!" (Jn 16:33).

fOR REflectiON

Jesus said, "Truly I tell you, there is no one who has left house or brothers or sisters or mother or father or children or fields, for my sake and for the sake of the good news, who will not receive a hundredfold now in this age—houses, brothers and sisters, mothers and children, and fields, with persecutions—and in the age to come eternal life (Mk 10:28–30).

In what way do I see consecrated chastity as a way of offering a total gift of myself to God and the people I serve?

"Those who in life choose continence for the kingdom of heaven do so...in view of the particular value connected with this choice and which must be discovered and welcomed personally as one's own vocation" (Pope John Paul II, General audience of March 10, 1982).

What values have I personally discovered in living chastity for the sake of the kingdom?

II

Celibacy and Community Life

THE TERM "VOW OF CELIBATE CHASTITY" SEEMS PREFERABLE TO "vow of chastity" because all are called to practice chastity according to their state, whether married or unmarried, lay, clerical or religious. "Celibate chastity" emphasizes that by the vow we promise to forego marriage and to live chaste lives as celibates for the sake of the kingdom of God, a special vocation to which God has called us. God's grace will help us to live our commitment faithfully, for sexuality is essential to our nature. Every human being, male or female, experiences strong desires to choose a spouse and have children. Nature strongly inclines us to sexual activity so that the human race will continue. But because of the effects of sin, most people find sex difficult to integrate. Thus a vow of celibacy faithfully lived gives a powerful witness of our commitment to God.

As mentioned in the previous chapter, St. Paul recommended celibacy as a means to free persons for total dedication to the things of God. Parents have all they can do to bring up their children, so they do not have the time or energy to take on the burdens of others as their main task. Taking a vow of celibacy and giving up spouse and family frees us to bear the burdens of those in God's family who have no one to help them. And why do we bear their burdens? To fulfill the law of Christ (cf. Gal 6:2).

The selfless Christlike love that parents show to spouse and children constitutes the holiness of the married state. But such dedication does not leave them with much leisure for prayer and contemplation. Good Christian parents pray earnestly for the grace to fulfill their obligations well, but finding time for regular prayer and contemplation can be a challenge.

Religious lead busy lives too, but our schedules include time for private prayer and liturgical prayer (the Eucharist and the Liturgy of the Hours). Our houses are usually quiet, unlike houses with children or teenagers, so that we can pray or meditate undisturbed, and we can often regulate our use of time more easily than parents can. Thus the vow of celibacy gives us a certain freedom for prayer and contemplation.

The vow enables us to grow in love, the ultimate goal of Christian life. Love directed to God expresses itself in prayer and adoration; love directed to our neighbor takes the form of compassionate service, especially for the needy. If celibacy does not make us more loving and Christlike, we are wasting our lives. St. Paul wrote: "If I give away all my possessions, and if I hand over my body so that I may boast, but do not have love, I gain nothing" (1 Cor 13:3). Unless it leads us to grow in Christlike love, our vow of celibacy will profit us nothing and could even harm us.

The analogy of a steam locomotive illustrates this. Fire stoked in its boiler turns water into steam, generating great internal pressure. If the steam escapes, the energy dissipates and no work gets done. If the steam stays bottled up, pressure builds up until it explodes, causing great damage. If the steam is properly released, it moves the pistons so that the engine can pull heavy trains for great distances.

Similarly, if sexual energy is properly used, it enriches human life. But if we do not harness our sexual energy we will waste it in frivolous pursuits and emotional displays, remaining immature and childish, tossed here and there by our unregulated emotions. We will never achieve the moral integrity and order in our emotional life that self-knowledge requires. Without moral virtue our self-knowledge and self-esteem will rest on a shaky foundation and so too will our love for others, for Jesus told us to love others as we love ourselves. Authentic self-possession and self-love (not selfishness) enables us to love others.

If, on the other hand, we suppress our sexual energy, this sets the stage for psychological problems. Our natural drives and emotions seek appropriate external expression. If they are repressed and given no outlet, the repression eventually causes inner tension that can cause violence, anger, self-pity, self-hatred, and hostility toward others. A vow of celibacy is not meant to repress our natural drives and emotions but to help us channel them in ways that enrich us and help us to better serve others in works of love (cf. Gal 5:13).

In the past, religious were taught to exert strict control over their feelings and emotions. Rules of behavior required us to keep our distance from one another and friendships were discouraged, as if strong friendships would harm the community. Warnings against "particular friendships" tended to obscure the value of true friendships.

Strong emotional and sexual attachments do indeed pose challenges to everyone. They are part of the reason people get married and commit themselves to each other for life, and they can be especially challenging to persons vowed to celibacy. But the difficulty is not removed by repression, by refusing to get close to anyone or by being unloving, but by loving everyone more, by loving as Christ loved us.

And how did Christ love us? As his friends. "No one has greater love than this, to lay down one's life for one's friends. You are my friends if you do what I command you" (Jn 15:13–14). A religious community should be a community of friends in the Lord, of those who love one another intensely from their hearts (1 Pet 1:22). Charity constitutes our best apostolic witness: "By this everyone will know that you are my disciples, if you have love for one another" (Jn 13:35).

The argument is clear enough:

- We advance the kingdom of God and show that we are disciples of Christ by loving as Christ loved us.
- Christ loved us as friends.
- Friends love one another intensely from their hearts.

So we advance the kingdom of God and act as disciples of Christ when we love one another intensely from our hearts. Such is the purpose of our vow of celibacy.

The vow is not meant to isolate us, for it is not good for human beings to be alone (Gen 2:18). Nor is it good for us celibates to live as strangers to each other. Religious communities grow in happiness, vitality, and productivity precisely when their members are all friends in the Lord.

But how are we to love one another intensely from our hearts and at the same time avoid the trap of exclusive friendships? Friendships become dangerous to celibates precisely when they are exclusive. Marital love is exclusive, for when a man loves a woman he wants this woman alone and no one else, and she wants him and no one else. Their exclusive love for each other ensures the stability of the family.

But friendships are not exclusive in that way. Good friends share common moral commitments and common interests, but they welcome others with the same commitments and interests into their circle.

Far from being exclusive, Christian charity is universal and unconditional, even extending to our enemies. If a friendship tends to exclusivity, if it pulls us away from our community rather than pulling us deeper into it, this clearly shows that we have lost balance and need to set things right.

Sunlight provides an analogy for love: when directed through a magnifying glass, the light burns whatever it focuses on. But when dispersed, the light brings trees and flowers into bloom. So too, when our love is concentrated on one person the flames of sexual passion can flare up and destroy our moral integrity and our union with God. But when our love is given freely, generously and selflessly to everyone, we bring them God's grace and blessing.

Although friendships can sometimes tend to become exclusive, we need not fear them. Quite the contrary. The love we have for our closest friends mirrors the love of Christ for all of us. Rather than live together in fearful isolation, true communion calls us to treat everyone with the warmth and openness normally reserved for our best friends. This provides an atmosphere most conducive to spiritual growth and deep internal peace and joy.

Being too reserved could pose a greater danger. At times we don't let people into our lives and then complain of loneliness. We won't ask for help and then complain of being overworked. We keep people at a distance and wonder why we feel empty, forgetting that in excluding others from our lives we are excluding God. For God dwells within us, and a person of deep faith reacts like John the Baptist in his mother's womb, who leaped for joy at the coming of Christ. Those who love as the Lord does are continually rejuvenated when others come to them. Yes, others bring us their troubles and may make additional work for us, but "where there is love there is no labor and if there is labor it is a labor of love" (St. Augustine). Love for God and neighbor renews us. Surely his love and compassion energized the Lord, for he never turned people away because he felt too tired. One of the most detailed stories in the Gospel describes Jesus' discussion with the Samaritan woman, whom Christ met at the well where he was resting from his fatigue (Jn 4:5–42). When the apostles returned with food and pressed him to eat he replied, "I have food to eat that you do not know about…. My food is to do the will of him who sent me and to complete his work" (Jn 4:32–34).

Do we open our hearts wide to others or do we keep people at a respectful distance? If we are insecure and don't believe we are lovable, then we may fear rejection. Perhaps in the past other people have hurt and disappointed us. Perhaps we feel we have nothing in common with some companions and don't find them interesting. We can find a thousand excuses for not reaching out to others in love, but Christian charity, which is unconditional, overrides them all. For the charity of Christ is friendly, open, welcoming, and generous, and so should ours be. St. Paul adds to the list when he writes: "Love is patient; love is kind; love is not envious or boastful or arrogant or rude. It does not insist on its own way; it is not irritable or resentful; it does not rejoice in wrongdoing, but rejoices in the truth. It bears all things, believes all things, hopes all things, endures all things. Love never ends. But as for prophecies, they will come to an end; as for tongues, they will cease; as for knowledge, it will come to an end" (1 Cor 13:4–8). That kind of love leaves no room for excuses. As celibates for the kingdom of God, our task is to live our lives fully and love as Christ loves us.

God loves each of us, no matter our shortcomings. He knows the hurts and traumas we have suffered. God shows us mercy because he knows us perfectly. He constantly calls us to step outside the shadow of evils that have darkened our lives and to venture into his marvelous light. When we open our hearts to one another, the healing of our past hurts begins. For other people can bear God's love to us. And as wounded healers, we can help them while they help us. Life in community with our celibate brothers or sisters provides a training ground for our apostolic work. Showing compassion for the difficult brothers or sisters we may live with in community can teach us to deal lovingly with the difficult people we meet in our apostolic work. This love and Christlike compassion renders our work apostolic, for the Lord has *sent* us to witness to his love.

Living the chaste, celibate life to which Christ has called us requires the courage to take up our cross every day to follow the Lord. It means directing the urgings of our nature and regulating our passions, as every chaste person is called to do. We take a vow of celibacy to enable us to love as Christ loved us. Thus St. Paul writes: "Welcome one another, therefore, just as Christ has welcomed you, for the glory of God" (Rom 15:7). Again, "Love one another with mutual affection; outdo one another in showing honor" (Rom 12:10). For when we open our hearts in love to all, as Christ did, then God is at home in us and we are at home in God and in our communities.

for Reflection

Therefore be imitators of God, as beloved children, and live in love, as Christ loved us and gave himself up for us, a fragrant offering and sacrifice to God. But fornication and impurity of any kind, or greed, must not even be mentioned among you, as is proper among saints. Entirely out of place is obscene, silly, and vulgar talk; but instead, let there be thanksgiving. Be sure of this, that no fornicator or impure person, or one who is greedy (that is, an idolater), has any inheritance in the kingdom of Christ and of God. Let no one deceive you with empty words, for because of these things the wrath of God comes on those who are disobedient. Therefore do not be associated with them. For once you were darkness, but now in the Lord you are light. Live as children of light—for the fruit of the light is found in all that is good and right and true (Eph 5:1–9).

How can community living be a help to living chastity? What can I contribute toward this goal?

Do I make an effort to cultivate good friendships? Is there anyone I could reach out to—someone who may need a friend?

12

Authority

THE GOSPELS OFTEN RECOUNT HOW THE APOSTLES COMPETED for status, for the first seats, for authority. Each time they bickered, Christ chided them for failing to understand his message and he explained how he expected them to act. For example, when the apostles came to him to ask who is the greatest, Jesus "called a child, whom he put among them, and said, 'Truly I tell you, unless you change and become like children, you will never enter the kingdom of heaven. Whoever becomes humble like this child is the greatest in the kingdom of heaven'" (Mt 18:2–4).

But they did not understand this lesson, for a little later the mother of James and John asked Jesus to promise that her two sons would sit on his right and on his left when he came into his kingdom. When the ten heard it, they grew angry with the two brothers. But Jesus called them to him and said:

> You know that the rulers of the Gentiles lord it over them, and their great ones are tyrants over them. It will not be so among you; but whoever wishes to be great among you must be your servant, and whoever wishes to be first among you must be your slave; just as the Son of Man came not to be served but to serve, and to give his life as a ransom for many (Mt 20:24–28).

St. Mark's Gospel relates a similar incident:

> Then they came to Capernaum; and when he was in the house he asked them, "What were you arguing about on the way?" But they were silent, for on the way they had argued with one another who was the greatest. He sat down, called the twelve, and said to them, "Whoever wants to be first must be last of all and servant of all" (Mk 9:33–35).

Our Lord dramatically illustrated this lesson for the apostles on the night before he died:

> The devil had already put it into the heart of Judas son of Simon Iscariot to betray him. And during supper Jesus, knowing that the Father had given all things into his hands, and that he had come from God and was going to God, got up from the table, took off his outer robe, and tied a towel around himself. Then he poured water into a basin and began to wash the disciples' feet and to wipe them with the towel that was tied around him (Jn 13:2–5).

Previous to this, Jesus had sent Peter and John to follow a man carrying a water jar and to prepare the Passover supper in the house he entered. As a mark of hospitality, hosts would wash the feet of guests who came to dinner. In a Jewish household, servants would perform this task, or the youngest child if the family had no servants. Though Peter and John had been sent to get things ready, it seems they didn't want to perform this task and neither did the other apostles. Why? Because whoever washed the feet of the others would clearly indicate that he was the lowest in rank, and none of them wanted to admit that. St. John's account continues:

> After he had washed their feet, had put on his robe, and had returned to the table, he said to them, "Do you know what I have done to you? You call me Teacher and

Lord—and you are right, for that is what I am. So if I, your Lord and Teacher, have washed your feet, you also ought to wash one another's feet. For I have set you an example, that you also should do as I have done to you. Very truly, I tell you, servants are not greater than their master, nor are messengers greater than the one who sent them. If you know these things, you are blessed if you do them" (Jn 13:12–17).[1]

Our Lord clearly taught that the greatest among his disciples is the one who most readily serves the needs of others and, like a child, does not seek special status. The more selfless we are, the more powerfully God can work through us. Thus the authority of a Christian, which comes from our union with God, differs from any other kind of authority and from authoritarianism and the need to control others.

For different kinds of authority exist. The authority of office is that which a person has while in office, but loses upon leaving office when another takes over. No matter how much power the office might confer, it ceases when the person completes the term of office.

Others possess the authority of knowledge. For example, doctors, scientists, or electricians are experts in their fields, and other people go to them for advice. Authority based on knowledge remains with the person for as long as he or she has that knowledge; it does not depend on office.

Persons of good character possess moral authority. Their

---

1. St. Luke places the teaching of Christ contained in Mt 18:3–4 in the setting of the Last Supper, where Luke says a dispute broke out regarding who of them "should be reckoned the greatest." Perhaps they were squabbling over the places they wanted to occupy at the table. He does not tell about Christ's washing the feet of the apostles but he seems to allude to it when he says "But not so with you; rather the greatest among you must become like the youngest" (Lk 22:26), for the youngest child washed the feet of guests.

actions reveal their moral integrity; they are not just good doctors or scientists but good persons. Good people have their lives in good order and habitually do what is right, living at peace with themselves. Others can look to them as models of good behavior and go to them for advice in making moral decisions.

Those who have made their own the teaching of Christ and live by it possess still another kind of authority. A moral person may practice virtue, but Christ commands us to go beyond merely keeping the natural law. He asks us to love our enemies and to pray for those who persecute us (cf. Mt 5:44). This love must not be mere show or lip service, hiding a deep-seated animosity and anger. Love does not allow us to act on angry and resentful feelings when some-one deliberately harms us, but makes us sad that someone could harm others. Love also makes us desire that the evil-doer may rise from the darkness of selfishness and sin to the joy and peace that Christ promises. We can admire and imitate persons who rise above unjust treatment and ill will and respond with genuine compassion for their enemies because they are acting as Jesus did. He wants his followers to have the authority that comes from a life lived in union with God and which manifests charity like his.

Jesus always amazed the crowds because he spoke with authority and not like the scribes and Pharisees. For Christ has the *authority of office*. His priesthood is eternal (cf. Heb 7:15–28). He is "the apostle and high priest of our confession" (Heb 3:1). For he came to reveal to us that God is our Father and to prove God's love for us by his death on the cross. He has the *authority of knowledge*: "No one knows the Father except the Son and anyone to whom the Son chooses to reveal him" (Mt 11:27). He has the *authority of a moral life.* "Which of you convicts me of sin?" he challenged his opponents (Jn 8:46). He has also *the authority of a holy life, of perfect, selfless, sacrificial love.* "No one has greater love than this, to lay down one's life for one's friends" (Jn 15:13). We will be "the light of the world" and have authority in the eyes of others when we love God and keep his word. Christ had such authority, and he wants us to show in our lives the authority of holiness, which urges us to serve all selflessly.

It took the apostles some time to learn this, for at first they wanted to lord it over others and make their authority felt. Such self-seeking gives a counter-witness to our Christian faith. Yet the desire for power can easily infect us. If we seek positions of authority to advance our careers, parade our works before others, think that we alone can fill a position because of our unique talents and training, or nourish anger and jealousy when others are chosen instead of us, then we do not have the kind of authority Christ wants us to have: the authority of holiness, of selfless, unconditional, all-embracing, compassionate, Christlike love, without which we are noisy gongs and clanging cymbals (cf. 1 Cor 13:1).

But does this mean we should not develop our talents? No, for if we treasure all God's gifts to us, we will develop them *so we can serve others better.* Should we pursue moral integrity? Of course, but remember that Christian love not only fulfills the law but transcends it, because God calls us to be loving even as our heavenly Father is loving (cf. Mt 5:48).

But if we desire a high office, we need to ask ourselves why. To lord it over others? But Christ has forbidden this. To confirm the good opinion we have (and want others to have) of ourselves? But charity does not boast and is not arrogant (cf. 1 Cor 13:4). To enjoy the rewards of high office?

But Christ told us to seek first the kingdom of God and his holiness (cf. Mt 6:33). The love of God should motivate us to serve others, not ourselves. If we desire positions of authority it should only be because they enable us to bear one another's burdens to fulfill the law of Christ. Although positions of authority may enable us to serve our neighbors better, they may not always do so.

Positions of authority that allow us to serve others in one way might also require us to forego other important services we might render in other ways. Recall Jotham's fable (Judg 9:7–21) about the trees wanting to choose a king. The olive tree, the fig tree, and the vine refused because they did not want to give up their fruit to stand swaying above the trees. When we assume positions of authority we often have to give up things we cherish (our teaching, pastoral ministry, research, nursing the sick, etc.). Those who make such sacrifices and serve us generously deserve our gratitude. But before abandoning old responsibilities to assume new ones we need to discern carefully where we can best serve, what we can bring to the position, and how our present assignment can be filled. This discernment calls us to collaborate with our superiors who assign us to our apostolic tasks. Boredom with our present duties or thinking our present assignment doesn't fully utilize all our talents are not good reasons for moving on. Every assignment has untold possibilities that require imagination and insight to discover, and hard work and generosity to develop. Other people have many needs, and the selfless, disciplined, and zealous person quickly discovers those needs and finds ways to meet them. We are rarely, if ever, too big for any job. No, we do not assume positions of authority to stand swaying above the trees but to serve others' needs. When we have this attitude the exercise of authority will not ensnare us with illusions of grandeur but will make us more humble and prayerful, conscious of our own limitations but confident that we can do all things in him who strengthens us (cf. Phil 4:13).

foR Reflection

Let every person be subject to the governing authorities; for there is no authority except from God, and those authorities that exist have been instituted by God. Therefore whoever resists authority resists what God has appointed, and those who resist will incur judgment. For rulers are not a terror to good conduct, but to bad. Do you wish to have no fear of the authority? Then do what is good, and you will receive its approval; for it is God's servant for your good. But if you do what is wrong, you should be afraid, for the authority does not bear the sword in vain! It is the servant of God to execute wrath on the wrongdoer (Rom 13:1–4).

What is my attitude toward authority? Do I see it as a means of service or as a status symbol?

How can I use whatever authority I may hold to serve others better?

13

the Vow of Obedience

THE WORD "OBEDIENCE" DERIVES FROM THE LATIN ROOT *audire*—to hear. This suggests that obedience calls for attentive listening. The virtue of obedience used to be explained as a complete willingness to do the will of the superior, who spoke with authority and did not generally ask for the input of the members. Today, in a more democratic age, community members participate in decision-making. Much consultation and dialogue take place before assent is asked and given. While some think that this new approach to obedience weakens religious authority, others see it as the best way to proceed when the decision reached will affect their lives. For religious are adults, not children to be told what to do. But after all the dialogue and consultation, who has the authority to make the final decision? In whom is that authority invested? Pope John Paul II has said:

> In the consecrated life the role of superiors, including local superiors, has always been of great importance for the spiritual life and for mission. In these years of change and experimentation, the need to revise this office has sometimes been felt. But it should be recognized that those who exercise authority *cannot renounce their obligation as those first responsible* for the community, as guides

of their brothers and sisters in the spiritual and apostolic life (*On Consecrated Life*, n. 43).

Through the vow of obedience, we vow to cooperate in the life and mission of our religious communities and agree to do what our superiors ask us to do. Clearly those in positions of responsibility will ask us to take on tasks according to our capabilities, so we can presume they have carefully considered our capacities, the demands of the work, and how our appointment will affect others. Superiors want our input about all this. They want to know our views and feelings about a new assignment, for they want us to be happy in doing it. But after the discussions have ended and superiors still choose us as the persons best suited for the task, we should go and do the best job we can. No matter how it is exercised, our vow of obedience requires us to obey.

We may think that obedience restricts our freedom, and in some senses it does. Being a member of any society requires us to obey its rules, for without rules society could not exist at all. Just as joining any society means giving up some freedom of action, so in entering a religious community, we bind ourselves in conscience to do generously whatever its authorities legitimately ask. In today's climate of autonomy, the vow of obedience highlights the true meaning of freedom:

> This obedience reproposes the obedience of Christ to the Father and, taking this mystery as its point of departure, testifies *that there is no contradiction between obedience and freedom*. Indeed, the Son's attitude discloses the mystery of human freedom as the path of obedience to the Father's will, and the mystery of obedience as the path to the gradual conquest of true freedom (*On Consecrated Life*, n. 91).

Our vow of obedience also makes community projects possible. We can found and maintain colleges, universities, parishes, hospitals, and nursing homes only because the community can assign members to work in these institutions. Due to declining membership, some religious communities are experiencing difficulty in maintaining a presence in their own institutions. Running stable apostolic works requires that the members will accept assignments to these works. Furthermore, when our superiors send us to do a certain work, we do not go merely as individuals acting on our own. We go as members of our religious community, realizing that our actions will affect not only our immediate apostolate but our community as well, and even the whole Church.

Religious men and women who vow to obey their religious superiors greatly benefit the Church, for they make possible the many institutions that serve the needs of the People of God. Members of religious communities were often the first to establish the Church in many parts of the world. They nurtured the first generations of believers by the faith communities and organizations they founded. Our vow of obedience helps us today to maintain many of the institutions that previous generations began.

Obedience also brings a great advantage to us as individual religious, even though we might prefer to follow our inclinations instead of obeying. Certainly we like to set goals, pursue our own courses of action, and take pride in what we achieve. But we are called to work as disciples of Christ, who has *commissioned* us to go out and to bear fruit that will last (cf. Jn 15:16). We have to be *sent* to perform any *apostolic* work. (The Greek word *apostellein* means "to send.") Thus Heb 3:1 calls Christ the "apostle and high priest of our confession" because he was sent by the Father.

Similarly, we are apostles when the community sends us; thus any apostolic work requires obedience. Like Christ we too want to say, "I seek to do not my own will but the will of him who sent me" (Jn 5:30).

Christ sends us to prepare others for his coming into their lives, and we can bring others to Christ only if we practice selfless love, which witnesses to the transforming power of divine love. This leaves no place for "pride of life," for self-centeredness can hinder our apostolate, whereas real charity enables us to make a sincere gift of ourselves to others. The true apostle takes on the attitude of John the Baptist, who said: "He must increase, but I must decrease" (Jn 3:30).

Christ told us that the seed must fall to the ground and die to produce much fruit. Only the humble shall possess the land (cf. Mt 5:5) and produce lasting fruit (cf. Jn 15:16). Our task is to labor; God will give the increase in his own good time. Working under obedience reminds us that our religious communities send us to do God's work and promote his kingdom, not to promote ourselves or advance our private interests. God sends us not to make a name for ourselves but to preach Christ and him crucified. Our vow of obedience helps us share in the obedience of Christ, who came not to do his own will but the will of the Father who sent him. That is why the obedient will share in the victory of Christ over sin, selfishness, and even death itself.

Our vow of obedience greatly benefits our apostolic ministry. It constitutes us as apostles, sent by our religious institutes and the Church, and safeguards us from "the pride of life" that can undermine our good motives, cloud our witness, and spoil our ministry. When the community sends us on an apostolic mission, our vow of obedience helps us grow in the awareness that we are sharing in the labors of fellow religious who founded, nurtured, and labored over the work now entrusted to us. In appreciation for the sacrifices they made we will treat that work with profound respect, making changes carefully lest we pull up wheat with the weeds, realizing how easily impatience or criticism can destroy the good already established. Of course changes will come, for we have to adapt to a changing world. But not all change brings progress. Conscious that our religious community has entrusted us with this work, we will make changes prudently and with careful discernment, never abruptly and insensitively. Our predecessors have long fostered close relationships with those we serve. A profound awareness of our responsibility to carry on that tradition will strengthen our community's witness and avoid misunderstandings with the laity.

How we act as religious reflects on our community. We should be friendly, accessible, compassionate but never condescending, welcoming but not overly familiar, never crossing the line into vulgarity or improper intimacy. Our vow of obedience helps us to remember that as religious priests, brothers, or sisters we need to uphold the honor and reputation of our institutes. What a terrible sin it would be to scandalize the faithful by immoral conduct! The vow of obedience helps us to remember that we represent not only our religious family, but Christ himself.

Many practical advantages follow from our vow of obedience. For as members of our religious institute, we have access to many talented and generous religious who can help us when needed. We can always turn to our religious family to receive generous assistance.

Obedience means listening to the Spirit, which also means to listen attentively to the requests of one another.

Because the work each does is a community work, all of us take an interest in it, pray for its success and contribute whatever help we can. As a family we try to support each other so no one feels lonely, isolated, or abandoned, even when we work at a distance from each other. As a community we also strive to discern the will of God together: "The fraternal life is the privileged place in which to discern and accept God's will, and to walk together with one mind and heart…. In community life which is inspired by the Holy Spirit, each individual engages in a fruitful dialogue with the others in order to discover the Father's will" (*On Consecrated Life*, n. 92).

In giving up our own projects to dedicate ourselves to the works of the community we gain much. It helps us to grow away from self-centeredness and open ourselves to the selfless love of Christ so that he can live and work in us. We gain the support, prayers, and encouragement of our community, which gives the witness Christ asks of us, so that when others see how we treat one another, they will be moved to remark, "See how those Christians love one another."

Acting under obedience, of course, things won't always go our way. Some decisions will disappoint us; sometimes we may suffer unfair treatment. We may even be removed before completing an important project or after our hard work has brought success. Such circumstances can cause us pain and tempt us to self-pity. In all honesty, superiors can make mistakes and do not always treat members with the respect and appreciation they deserve. But dwelling on being "victimized" in this way can make us exaggerate the injustice done to us and foster anger and resentment. But perhaps God allows these things to happen for our spiritual growth.

Such treatment can remind us that we exercise an apostolate only as sent by our religious family, for we have no "private apostolate." If we harbor resentment and lick our wounds in self-pity, much of our preceding "apostolic" work probably had far more self-seeking than we realized. For, as St. Paul writes: "Love is patient; love is kind; love is not envious or boastful or arrogant or rude. It does not insist on its own way; it is not irritable or resentful; it does not rejoice in wrongdoing, but rejoices in the truth. It bears all things, believes all things, hopes all things, endures all things. Love never ends" (1 Cor 13:4–8).

Even if we were wronged, we can choose not to let somebody else's failure diminish our lives. Even in difficult circumstances a person of faith will believe that "all things work together for good for those who love God" (Rom 8:28). The important thing is to love and then wait to see the good emerge. Then even if our work suffers in the short term, *we* will not suffer harm. We will grow in faith, hope, and love and do God's work even more effectively, having been purified in our disappointment. In our future apostolic work we will not hinder God's grace by our selfishness. The obedient shall share in the victory of Christ, who has conquered the world by his perfectly selfless love (cf. Jn 16:33).

for Reflection

In the days of his flesh, Jesus offered up prayers and supplications, with loud cries and tears, to the one who was able to save him from death, and he was heard because of his reverent submission. Although he was a Son, he learned obedience through what he suffered; and having been made perfect, he became the source of eternal salvation for all who obey him (Heb 5:7–9).

Do I know how to really *listen?*

What does obedience have to say to a culture that puts unqualified value on individual autonomy?

14

Disagreements, Discussion, and Community Building

*T*HOUGH COMPOSED OF MANY DIFFERENT INDIVIDUALS, RELIGIOUS communities, like other human organizations, are unified by a common purpose. Just as a team succeeds when its members coordinate their individual efforts to win, so a religious community can flourish only when all its members cooperate in working toward the same goal. We will stay united by keeping in mind the ultimate goal that Christ has established for each of us: holiness of life—loving as Christ has loved us. In this way we show ourselves children of our heavenly Father who is love (cf. 1 Jn 3:18–19; 4:8).

By making our vows in our religious institutes, we have committed ourselves to cooperate with one another in forming such ideal Christian communities that those who observe us will say, "See how these Christians love one another." Such witness leads others to the Lord. To achieve unity constantly challenges us, for religious have different opinions on many issues, as might be expected among men and women of different races, cultures, ages, and training. This diversity contributes to the richness and vitality of any community, but it can also foster division and disunity. St. Paul warns of the disagreements and factions that can arise in a Christian community if the members become self-indulgent (cf. Gal 5:13–21). We know the dangers and we also know the love, joy and peace that the Spirit brings into our lives (cf. Gal 5:22). We can face dangers with confidence knowing that Christ has overcome the world (cf. Jn 16:33).

Yet conflicts still arise. Even the apostles bickered over who of them was the most important, so that Christ had to rebuke them. Even after the Holy Spirit had come upon them, they still argued. For example, after many years of fruitful collaboration, St. Paul and St. Barnabas disagreed so sharply that they decided to split up and preach the Gospel separately (cf. Acts 15:36–40).

But far more serious disputes threatened the unity of the early Christian community. Let us briefly review some of these problems and see how the Church resolved them, to discover a model for resolving serious disputes that may threaten our unity.

Although our Lord had occasionally preached in Samaria and Syro-Phoenicia, he confined his main efforts to the House of Israel and told his disciples to do the same (cf. Mt 10:5–6). At the ascension he told them they would be his witnesses "in Jerusalem, in all Judea and Samaria, and to the ends of the earth" (Acts 1:8). The mission to the Gentiles began with St. Peter's baptism of the household of Cornelius, who had been told in a vision to send someone to Jaffa to find a man named Peter (cf. Acts 10). Before the people whom Cornelius had sent arrived, Peter had a vision of a sheet filled with various kinds of animals. As the sheet was let down by its corners from heaven, a voice told Peter: "Kill and eat." Peter refused to eat anything unclean and the voice said, "What God has made clean, you must not call profane" (Acts 10:15). This was repeated three times and the sheet was then drawn up to heaven. When the delegation arrived Peter welcomed them, and the next day he accompanied them to the home of Cornelius. While he spoke to them about Jesus, the Holy Spirit descended on them so Peter had them all baptized, even though they were Gentiles.

Peter's actions shocked the Church in Jerusalem. How could he eat with Gentiles and even baptize them? When they demanded an explanation, Peter told them about the events that led to the conversion of the household of Cornelius. Hearing this, the members of the Church praised God.

Later some Gentiles were converted in Antioch and Barnabas went to assess the situation. Then he went to Tarsus to find Paul and together they established the Christian community there. But another controversy arose concerning the question: Do Gentile Christians have to observe the Law of Moses? Some members of the Church in Jerusalem had gone to Antioch and told the Gentile converts that they had to keep the law of Moses. St. Paul vehemently opposed this faction in a meeting in Jerusalem, which settled the question in Paul's favor (cf. Gal 2:1–10). Acts 15 tells us how the early Church resolved this dispute:

> Then certain individuals came down from Judea and were teaching the brothers, "Unless you are circumcised according to the custom of Moses, you cannot be saved." And after Paul and Barnabas had no small dissension and debate with them, Paul and Barnabas and some of the others were appointed to go up to Jerusalem to discuss this question with the apostles and the elders.... But some believers who belonged to the sect of the Pharisees stood up and said, "It is necessary for them to be circumcised and ordered to keep the law of Moses."

The apostles and the elders met together to consider this matter. After there had been much debate, Peter stood up and said to them, "My brothers, you know that in the early days God made a choice among you, that I should be the one through whom the Gentiles would hear the message of the good news and become believers.... We believe that we will be saved through the grace of the Lord Jesus, just as they will (Acts 15:1–2, 5–7, 11).

Notice that they had a long and heated argument in Antioch and neither side would give in, so they sent Paul and Barnabas to Jerusalem to *discuss* the problem with the other apostles. Paul and Barnabas reported their success among the Gentile converts, showing their opponents how strongly the faith had taken hold among them.

But the party of converted Pharisees insisted that the new Gentile converts should be circumcised and instructed to keep the Law of Moses. What happened next? The apostles met to discuss the situation, and they debated a long time. Notice neither side gave in without a fight, prolonging the debate. When they had thoroughly examined the question, they came to a consensus and reached a decision. Then Peter recapped the discussions and stated their decision. The apostles and elders fully agreed with Paul. Justification comes through faith in Jesus Christ. After this, "The whole assembly kept silence, and listened to Barnabas and Paul as they told of all the signs and wonders that God had done through them among the Gentiles" (Acts 15:22).

Finally, James spoke. By appealing to the prophet Amos to confirm what the Church had decided, he was clearly showing that the Jewish tradition itself prophesied about this opening to the Gentiles. He then proposed dietary rules that would not set Jewish and Gentile Christians apart from each other, but from pagan ritual practices.

What can we learn from their story? First we can expect that community members will often disagree, for people can have very strong opinions.

Second, the community strives to arrive at a consensus through careful, serious discussions, and this may take a long time. Discussing our disagreements helps build community, because we examine the issues that seem to divide us in light of the goals and ideals that unite us. This calls for patience, because matters are not usually resolved quickly. St. Luke tells us that the discussions in Jerusalem went on a long time.

Third, after they had reached a consensus, Peter articulated the fundamental and deciding issue: that we are all "saved through the grace of the Lord Jesus" (Acts 15:11). Similarly, the superior articulates the consensus of the community.

Fourth, reaching a final decision closes the matter. No rehashing old arguments, no complaining, no ill will, but full acceptance and cooperation. Just as the apostles tried to discover where the Spirit was leading them, so we try to find out too.

Fifth, such meetings call for respecting the opinions and feelings of others. No ridicule, no personal attacks, no *ad hominem* arguments, no highly emotional diatribes—nothing that would wound the feelings or consciences of others. To win an argument but fracture the community in the process makes everyone suffer. As a source of healing, not dissension, these meetings call for kindness and charity. Unfair tactics, cutting remarks, or political strategies and cliques are out of place. No one person has the only right solution, so open-minded listening and discussion will allow the truth to emerge.

Lastly, remember that the issues we have to decide are not as momentous as the problems the early Church faced. If our solution is less than perfect, we can later reassess our decision as new information arises. But notice that the community decides the question. The superior convenes the community, conducts the meeting, moderates the discussion, and articulates the consensus. Then we can depart in silence, charity, and peace.

for Reflection

> But when Cephas came to Antioch, I opposed him to his face, because he stood self-condemned; for until certain people came from James, he used to eat with the Gentiles. But after they came, he drew back and kept himself separate for fear of the circumcision faction. And the other Jews joined him in this hypocrisy, so that even Barnabas was led astray by their hypocrisy. But when I saw that they were not acting consistently with the truth of the gospel, I said to Cephas before them all, "If you, though a Jew, live like a Gentile and not like a Jew, how can you compel the Gentiles to live like Jews?" (Gal 2:11–14)

What is my attitude toward the ideas of others?

How do I handle conflict?

What would help me to speak the truth in charity?

15

Dialogue

THE SECOND VATICAN COUNCIL HAS PROFOUNDLY AFFECTED the concept of authority in the Church. Ever since the First Vatican Council defined the infallibility of the pope, papal authority was so emphasized that the authority of local bishops was almost overlooked. The Church was viewed as the kingdom of God upon earth with the pope as its visible head. But Vatican II strove to find a better balance between papal authority and that of the bishops. While reaffirming the supreme authority of the pope, the Council emphasized the local authority of the bishops and their collegiality as successors of the apostles. Each bishop has a certain autonomy and a corresponding responsibility for the whole Church, now viewed as the People of God. Modern thought, which stresses the rights and responsibilities of the individual, has strongly affected our ways of thinking. Even in religious communities individuals demand to be heard. The age of dialogue has come upon us.

Yet dialogue has always been part of church life, as the many ecumenical and local councils attest. Religious orders and congregations have used dialogue for centuries; the rules of many religious communities called for local chapters (meetings) where opinions were debated. Today chapters still provide important forums for discussion, often in a manner much less structured than before. Dialogue forms an important ingredient of religious houses throughout the world.

Houses of formation prepare candidates to live in community while training them for their later work. Community living demands much of us, and effective formation teaches us to face these demands squarely and accept them willingly. Chapter meetings provide an effective means for improving our community life and for preparing us for the give and take of life in the modern world. A local chapter gives us an occasion for sharing our common problems in the informal manner of a family gathering. This family spirit helps us draw fruit from these discussions as we sit down together as brothers and sisters, as friends in the Lord.

These discussions are certainly not weapons to be used against authority, nor ways of squeezing concessions from the superior. Such tactics would hardly make us grow in the virtue of obedience. Nor does giving vent to bitter and angry criticism help build up the community.

What purpose do these discussions have? They provide forums to exchange views and to air opinions regarding mutual problems in living religious life. This exchange helps everyone to understand the problems better. Then, by joint effort, perhaps the community will find good solutions. These discussions also help to foster a spirit of unity and cooperation in the house, besides serving many purposes:

a) First of all, in formation to religious life and the priesthood complex problems often arise, so the community can benefit from the counsel of everyone. All community members have the right to express their opinions, for the Spirit works in everyone, even the young and inexperienced. St. Benedict expressly tells the abbot to consult the community, even the youngest member. Scripture tells us that in the new dispensation, under which we are living, "your sons and your daughters shall prophesy, your old men shall dream dreams, and your young men shall see visions" (Joel 2:28; cf. Acts 2:17).

b) Bringing problems out into the open helps everyone realize what the community faces. Being aware of the problem makes us more willing to cooperate in finding a solution. So we more quickly develop a sense of corporate responsibility, prudence, and concern for the good of the house. Although confidential matters need to be kept private, not sharing problems that concern the whole community can easily cause a dichotomy to develop between superiors and members. Each group may begin to talk about "us" and "them," whereas a family talks only about "us." As a result, the community spirit may break down as individuals grow indifferent toward the group. Then those in authority are forced to bear the burden of maintaining a sense of community, thus losing one of the greatest advantages of religious life: bonding, the inestimable value of mutual support and edification. Dialogue helps us to give the witness of unity that Christ wants of us. Discussing community problems together draws us closer. Without it we tend to go our solitary ways.

Many years ago I saw the movie "I Remember Mama." The whole family gathered around the kitchen table every Friday night. Mama would call out the bills and Father would take out the corresponding amount of money from his pay envelope until all the bills were accounted for. Sometimes they had to rearrange things if a big bill was due and they did not have enough money on hand to pay it.

Then last of all, Mama would say, "Good, now we do not have to go to the bank." As the children later learned, the family had no money in the bank. But facing their problems together drew them closer and they felt secure. Families share problems, helping each other out. As brothers and sisters in Christ, shouldn't we do the same?

c) Dialogue offers a powerful means of formation. Studies of colleges have shown that the most powerful force in forming the students' mentality is not the faculty, but the students themselves. Dormitory discussions and exchanges over coffee or snacks form attitudes, values, and viewpoints. I think this also occurs in formation houses. A spirit of criticism can easily erupt when a few articulate critics start complaining. Conversely, the quiet witness of one person totally dedicated to selfless love and service can inspire everyone. Our conversations with each other help us form attitudes toward prayer and the vows.

Dialogue in formation certainly has great importance. The following suggestions offer some ways of using it wisely:

a) Presenting our opinions in a calm and objective way lets our reasons speak for themselves. Avoiding inflammatory language helps to focus greater light on the issues and facilitate listening and understanding.

b) Speaking with humility and charity will help keep the discussion on track. As St. Francis de Sales so aptly said, "Truth which is not charitable springs from a charity which is not true." In discussions, as in most things, practice perfects our skill, so we need patience with ourselves if our efforts fall short. Without trying to force our suggestions on others nor to embarrass or belittle them, we will try our best to be patient and understand each other's views. Disagreeing with another's argument calls for exquisite tact and consummate kindness, keeping in mind St. Paul's advice to Timothy: "convince, rebuke, and encourage, with the utmost patience in teaching" (2 Tim 4:2).

c) The importance of listening can't be stressed too much—a closed heart, a closed mind; an open heart, an open mind. We need to listen not only to the words others say but to the unspoken feelings that underlie their remarks. Listening with open hearts will foster a true dialogue, where no one dominates the meeting. These discussions can help to solve problems and lead us to understand each other better, fostering greater unity. Even in talking about issues that evoke strong feelings, dialogue calls for a receptive attitude to other people and their views.

d) Dialogue helps us to avoid classifying those who disagree with us, which can easily lead to factions. Branding others as the "opposition" makes it very difficult to judge fairly whatever they say. Instead of seeing a friend in the Lord speaking, we see an opponent. But because all persons are made in God's image, we must respect their right to their opinions, even if we disagree. To treat others with charity takes precedence over all else.

We often base our decisions more on feelings than on purely rational grounds, for our emotional states greatly influence our judgments. So too in discussing mutual problems, a meeting of minds calls for a meeting of hearts. For the Holy Spirit of truth leads us to the complete truth (cf. Jn 16:13). Stressing the things that bind us together fosters greater unity. If we were not united on the really important matters, we would not remain in our religious communities devoting our lives to serve Christ and his Church. We differ only in accidental matters. As the First Letter of Peter reminds us: "Above all, maintain constant love for one another, for love covers a multitude of sins" (1 Pet 4:8). A union of hearts fosters the meeting of minds.

Cultivating a spirit of dialogue in our religious houses brings many advantages both for our life together now and for our work later on. The laity are assuming a much more active role in the Church today than they did formerly. Priests, brothers, and sisters today must learn to solicit the ideas, viewpoints, and help of the laity. It is an extremely effective way of involving them in the life of the parish or school. Deeply religious people lacking in formal education may have profound insights based on their personal experience of living the Gospel. The better educated may have professional expertise that can benefit our apostolic work. Even good people who do not share our Catholic faith can help us in our work.

A spirit of friendly discussion and dialogue will help us to develop unity, to live together in peace and harmony, to grow into a real community. Although made up of individuals with different mental and physical characteristics, different backgrounds, attitudes and outlooks, we can all help one another to pursue holiness and to love as Christ has loved us. A spirit of open, friendly dialogue will help make us what Christ calls us to be — truly Christian communities, united in mind and heart.

St. Paul has some timely advice:

> But we appeal to you, brothers and sisters, to respect those who labor among you, and have charge of you in the Lord and admonish you; esteem them very highly in love because of their work. Be at peace among yourselves. And we urge you, beloved, to admonish the idlers, encourage the faint hearted, help the weak, be patient with all of them. See that none of you repays evil for evil, but always

seek to do good to one another and to all. Rejoice always, pray without ceasing, give thanks in all circumstances; for this is the will of God in Christ Jesus for you (1 Thess 5:12–18).

ꜰⱺʀ ʀefʟeᴄᴛioɴ

If then there is any encouragement in Christ, any consolation from love, any sharing in the Spirit, any compassion and sympathy, make my joy complete: be of the same mind, having the same love, being in full accord and of one mind. Do nothing from selfish ambition or conceit, but in humility regard others as better than yourselves. Let each of you look not to your own interests, but to the interests of others (Phil 2:1–4).

What do I consider as open-minded listening?

What steps can I take to understand others' points of view, even if I disagree with them?

Do I usually put my own interests ahead of the interests of others?

16

Living and talking with god

FROM MY EARLIEST DAYS I WAS ENCOURAGED TO LIVE IN THE presence of God, but this practice was stressed the most during my novitiate. Our whole life as novices fostered a prayerful attitude. We lived a very simple life, following a regular daily schedule: Mass and Office, private prayer, meditation, spiritual reading, study of religious life and the vows, and a few hours of manual labor. We spent most of the day in silence, with spiritual reading at meals. Community recreation took place only after the noon and evening meals. Having no contact with the outside world meant few outside distractions. If we were ever to learn to live in the presence of God, we would most likely succeed during the novitiate.

Returning to university life brought an abrupt transition: all the excitement of study along with the pressure to write papers and to do well on examinations. Facing the "real" world with all its obligations meant concentrating on the work at hand, while still finding time in our busy schedules for prayer, spiritual reading, and meditation. A dichotomy arose between prayer and work. The practice of the presence of God began to look like a pious but impractical ideal, well-meant but unrealistic, a practice to be abandoned lest it cause undue anxiety and feelings of guilt.

But to abandon the practice may make us forget that we are temples of the Holy Spirit who dwells in us and with us (cf. Jn 14:17; 1 Cor 3:16–17). If we separate our prayer and our work, how will our work be apostolic? I would like to suggest a way to avoid this dilemma.

Students entering the university choose a major and then select their courses in view of that initial commitment, which unifies and gives meaning to all their studies. The strength of that commitment also gives them the determination they need to do well in their courses, especially the more difficult ones. The same is true of the moral life. Once we have committed ourselves to be good persons of strong moral character, we ought to always act in ways befitting a human being. We are then prepared to practice whatever virtue a particular situation calls for. Our determination to be morally upright is then expressed in the right order we impose on our emotions and our actions. The practice of virtue challenges us more at the beginning of our efforts, but in time good habits (virtues) develop and we do what is right with ease, consistency, and delight.

In the spiritual life, the life of faith, Christ calls us to grow in holiness as our heavenly Father is holy (cf. Mt 5:48). Besides regulating our desires and passions and practicing the moral virtues like honesty and justice, we are to love as Christ loved us. As Christians and religious we commit ourselves to love God with our whole heart and soul and our neighbor as ourselves (cf. Lk 10:27). *The more this basic commitment influences our lives, the more we will live in the presence of God.*

Virtue always challenges us: to be generous when others are not, to refrain from unkindly retorting to a critical remark, to turn the other cheek and walk the extra mile (cf. Mt 5:39, 41). In such situations when our commitment to virtue conflicts with our natural inclinations, only our love of God will give us the strength to behave as children of God. In our weakness we cry to God for help but we do not have to cry aloud, for God dwells in the depths of our hearts.

But recalling God's presence is not only for difficult moments, because God has given us all the good things in our lives: our life, health, and talents, the goodness in other people, the beauty of nature. Seeing all these good things as his gifts moves us to thank God for them, practicing in our own lives the advice of St. Paul: "Be thankful" (Col 3:15).

We can give thanks even when the pressures of our work and the bustle and frantic pace of our lives pull us apart. For these things often force us to seek God's help in setting our priorities and making good decisions. God, in brief, becomes our constant companion, our counselor, our confidant.

Living in the presence of God, our constant companion, comes about when we sincerely want to do his will in everything and base our decisions on his will. Although our busy and often hectic lives make it difficult, doing God's will gives order, direction, and meaning to our lives. It helps us look beneath the surface of things to discover their deeper meaning. As our focus on life grows clearer and our conflicting desires are brought into line, we experience less inner turmoil and more inner peace—the peace that the world cannot give. This peace comes from our awareness of God's presence and our certitude born of experience that "all things work together for good for those who love God, who are called according to his purpose" (Rom 8:28).

As our lives become more rooted in God who dwells within us, a shift in our prayer often occurs. As we come to realize that God knows us even better than we know ourselves, our prayer becomes simple, trusting, and even wordless.

Our prayer is simple because we stand before God as we are, with no disguises. Putting aside all pretenses and excuses helps us to pray humbly and honestly, like the tax collector who went up to the temple and prayed, "God, be merciful to me, a sinner" (Lk 18:13). But unlike the tax collector we dare to raise our eyes to God, for he is our Father and our failures give us a greater claim upon his compassion.

Our prayer is trusting and confident because we know that as our constant companion God knows what we need even before we ask him. He has promised that if we seek his kingdom and his righteousness first, he will take care of all our needs (Mt 6:32–33). We don't have to pester God with endless requests, but simply to ask for our daily bread. As our Father he wants only the best for us, so we pray that his will be done on earth as it is in heaven (cf. Mt 6:7–13).

Finally, our prayer becomes wordless, for deep love and perfect trust don't require words. A happily married couple doesn't always need to talk about their love; they only need to be together. Sometimes words only intrude. So it is in our relationship with God.

> Likewise the Spirit helps us in our weakness; for we do not know how to pray as we ought, but that very Spirit intercedes with sighs too deep for words. And God, who searches the heart, knows what is the mind of the Spirit, because the Spirit intercedes for the saints according to the will of God. We know that all things work together for good for those who love God, who are called according to his purpose (Rom 8:26–28).

With wordless and quiet prayer we can rest in the Lord's presence, better prepared to listen to him. The Lord wants this, but we often let other concerns preoccupy us. He wants us to cast our burdens on him and let him sustain us (cf. 1 Pet 5:7). Christ's visit to the home of Martha, Mary, and Lazarus teaches us this important lesson. "Mary sat at the Lord's feet and listened to him speaking." Martha complained that Mary had left her to do all the work of serving the meal. But Christ defended Mary for having chosen the better part (cf. Lk 10:38–42).

This story is sometimes explained as proving the contemplative life superior to the active life. But this hardly seems to be its intent. After all, Christ considers as done to himself whatever we do for the least of his brethren, and he rewards us for it. He would certainly appreciate Martha's efforts and the gracious hospitality this family must have often offered him. What does he want to teach us?

Our Lord told us that he had not come to be served but to serve, and though he appreciated the hospitality this family offered so lovingly and generously, he was also coming to their house to serve them, to provide for their needs. Preoccupied with much serving, Martha was *too busy* to listen to Christ. Mary sat at his feet and listened to him; she had indeed chosen the better part. While Martha felt anxious and preoccupied, Mary was at peace.

In the Gospels Christ often says "Come to me." What does he mean? In John's Gospel Christ says, "Everyone who has heard and learned from the Father comes to me" (Jn 6:45); "Whoever is from God hears the words of God" (Jn 8:47); and "Those who love me will keep my word, and my Father will love them, and we will come to them and make our home with them" (Jn 14:23). God wants us to listen to him in the depths of our heart where he dwells in us (cf. Jn 15:4) and to bring our problems to him, as he told us to do: "Come to me, all you that are weary and are carrying heavy burdens, and I will give you rest" (Mt 11:28). Placing our burdens at his feet, we then listen to what he has to tell us.

In the quiet moments when, like Mary, we sit at Our Lord's feet and listen to him, he refreshes and renews us. For in listening to God who speaks to us not only in prayer and quiet reflection but also as we labor, we learn what he wants us to do. We draw ever closer to him and he to us. When we shoulder once more the burdens of our apostolic life, we do so with a peace that the world cannot give or take away (cf. Jn 14:27). Then our occupations never become preoccupations, for we realize we are doing his work and that God will work more effectively through us if we listen to him. The apostles worked hard all one night on their own and caught nothing, but following the Lord's directions they caught so many fish they could not haul them into the boat. They had to drag the nets to shore where Christ served them breakfast (cf. Jn 21:1–14).

To live in the presence of God doesn't mean thinking about him all day, but to *commit ourselves* to do God's will in all things. Hence we learn to heed his inspirations, to seek his advice, help, and encouragement. This leads to inner growth, for God dwells in the hearts of all who believe in him. The greater our union with God, the less our problems will burden us. Yes, the love of Christ impels us to take on the burdens of others, but because we assume them at Christ's bidding they are *his* burdens. He will help us carry them: "Take my yoke upon you, and learn from me; for I am gentle and humble in heart, and you will find rest for your souls. For my yoke is easy, and my burden is light" (Mt 11:29–30). No matter how busy our lives, to the degree that we live in the presence of God and do his will, we are preparing ourselves for prayer. When we are finally free to lay our burdens at his feet and turn our full attention to him in prayer, we will be ready to receive his grace and he will fill us with his love, peace, and joy.

fOR Reflection

Abide in me as I abide in you. Just as the branch cannot bear fruit by itself unless it abides in the vine, neither can you unless you abide in me. I am the vine, you are the branches. Those who abide in me and I in them bear much fruit, because apart from me you can do nothing. Whoever does not abide in me is thrown away like a branch and withers; such branches are gathered, thrown into the fire, and burned. If you abide in me, and my words abide in you, ask for whatever you wish, and it will be done for you (Jn 15:4–7).

They urged him [Jesus] strongly, saying, "Stay with us, because it is almost evening and the day is now nearly over." So he went in to stay with them. When he was at the table with them, he took bread, blessed and broke it, and gave it to them. Then their eyes were opened, and they recognized him; and he vanished from their sight. They said to each other, "Were not our hearts burning within us while he was talking to us on the road, while he was opening the scriptures to us?" (Lk 24:29–32).

Do I realize that God is always present with me, even if it doesn't feel like it?

How can I live in a greater awareness of God's presence?

17

Learning to pray

AS AN ITINERANT RABBI, JESUS JOURNEYED FROM TOWN TO town throughout the hilly, rugged terrain of the Holy Land. The road between Jericho and Jerusalem climbs about 2,700 feet above sea level, winding steeply through the barren hills of the Judean desert. To reach the towns perched on the hillsides, travelers had to climb unpaved country lanes that grew dusty in the dry season and muddy in the wet. Christ referred to the hardships of his life when he told the scribe who wanted to follow him: "Foxes have holes, and birds of the air have nests; but the Son of Man has nowhere to lay his head" (Mt 8:19).

On another occasion, tired from his journey through Samaria, Jesus rested by a well while his disciples went to buy food. As he waited for them, he met a Samaritan woman (cf. Jn 4:1–42). Christ did not get much rest on that occasion or on many others. The crowds in Capernaum pressed upon him so that he and his disciples could hardly eat (cf. Mk 3:20). Mothers brought their children so he could touch them (cf. Lk 18:15). His relatives could not get to him because of the crowds (cf. Lk 8:19). Even when Jesus crossed the lake to rest, crowds followed, and he preached to them (cf. Mk 6:30–35). Although he constantly traveled and preached, Jesus often went by himself into the hills to pray through the night (cf. Lk 6:12).

Once when the apostles went to look for him and found him praying, his deep concentration and reverence must have impressed them. They did not dare to intrude but waited until he had finished. Then one of his disciples said, "Lord, teach us to pray." In this setting St. Luke records the Lord's prayer (cf. Lk 11:1–4). St. Matthew's Gospel, instead, places the Lord's prayer in the Sermon on the Mount, where Christ first tells us how *not* to pray. What advice did he give us on prayer?

He tells us first not to pray to impress others, for we pray to get in touch with God. The Lord invites us to disregard all other thoughts and enter into the secret, inner chambers of our heart where God dwells (cf. Jn 14:23; 1 Cor 3:16–17; 6:19), to commune with him peacefully and quietly.

Jesus tells us, "When you are praying, do not heap up empty phrases as the Gentiles do; for they think that they will be heard because of their many words" (Mt 6:7). Prayer does not try to overwhelm God with a torrent of words. Christ assures us that he knows our needs even before we ask (cf. Mt 6:8). In prayer, we first put ourselves in God's presence, adopting a peaceful attitude. God wants us to feel at home with him, for he is at home with us (cf. Jn 15:4). Dwelling in God, we enjoy peace. A prayerful spirit helps us to *listen* to him, for the Holy Spirit dwells in us to remind us of all Christ has taught us (cf. Jn 14:26). He taught that God our Father loves us unconditionally and always wants our good. So we pray with the confidence that comes from knowing that "all things work together for good for those who love God, who are called according to his purpose"

(Rom 8:28). With reverence and peace, we prayerfully focus on God, eager to tell him our needs and listen to his inspirations, confident that he will show us how to profit from our difficulties.

In the opening words of the Lord's prayer, Jesus taught us this attitude of reverent, loving, confident communion with our heavenly Father: "Our Father in heaven, hallowed be your name. Your kingdom come. Your will be done, on earth as it is in heaven" (Mt 6:9–10). In devoutly praying these words, we raise our minds and hearts to God in reverence, confidence, love, and adoration.

What do we talk to God about? We pray for our daily bread, for everything needed to live as his children and as disciples of his Son. But Christ has told us not to "live by bread alone, but by every word that comes from the mouth of God" (Mt 4:4), for he is the bread of life, and whoever comes to him will never hunger (cf. Jn 6:35). Praying with this in mind, how many of our worries and concerns diminish! We begin to see that so many of our "needs" are not real needs but wants, and these wants may not truly benefit us. In prayer, these artificial wants lose their grip on us and we gain greater freedom and peace. God will give us what we really need, if we only "seek first the kingdom of God and his holiness," and put aside all worry (Mt 6:33–34). Our Lord asks us to pray with utter confidence in God, casting our cares upon him, knowing he is looking after us (cf. 1 Pet 5:7). Such an attitude helps us to discover and to do his will.

In realizing the Lord's loving concern and great compassion for us, we also become profoundly aware of our selfishness and sin. We see clearly that his great love demands that we love and forgive others as he loves and forgives us. By forgiving those who have offended us, our hearts will enlarge, making us more open to others. Prayerful communion with God dissolves all bitterness, hatred, and revenge, flooding our hearts with peace.

Prayer makes us realize that we can do all things in him who strengthens us (cf. Phil 4:13). At the same time, it makes us profoundly aware that of ourselves and unsupported by God's grace, we would fail at the first temptation. So we ask God not to allow us to be tempted but to protect us from evil.

The Lord's prayer perfectly expresses our relationship to God: reverence, love, confidence, humility, serenity, and open-hearted acceptance of others. For God will never allow us to be tempted beyond our capacity (cf. 1 Cor 10:13); adversities and trials will always benefit us if we remain in touch with him. For despite their power, ocean storms rage only on the surface. The deep currents move on unaffected by the surface turmoil. So it happens with us. By praying as the Lord taught us we enter into the center of our hearts and silently adore God, listening like Mary sitting at the Lord's feet. In this way we come to realize he speaks words of peace, not affliction. Prayer thus restores our peace of mind, rekindles our love, and strengthens our confidence. As Jesus said, "I have said this to you, so that in me you may have peace. In the world you face persecution. But take courage; I have conquered the world!" (Jn 16:33). Our faith in God as Father triumphs over everything: "This is the victory that conquers the world, our faith" (1 Jn 5:1).

But what do we do when our faith grows weak? When God seems distant and he doesn't seem to be listening to us? When prayer feels like we are only talking to ourselves? When we suspect that prayer is only an effort to convince ourselves that everything will work out, despite mounting problems and meager resources? What do we do when our problems so agitate us that they disturb our inner peace?

When worries weigh us down and doubts and fears torment us, we can admit them honestly, articulate them as best we can, and talk to the Lord about them. The Lord wants to hear about our doubts and weakness of faith, about our worries and our inability to let go of them. Our weakness and misery can become the topic of our prayer. We can only come before the Lord as we are. In the Gospel, the blind, the lame, and the sick knew of their conditions and brought them to the Lord. Even the man who had only weak faith cried out, "I believe, help my unbelief" (Mk 9:24). He was praying for his son out of desperation. They all did what St. Peter tells us to do: "Cast all your anxiety on him, because he cares for you" (1 Pet 5:8).

In prayer we don't fight ourselves but unburden ourselves on the Lord. When our burdens, problems, and doubts overwhelm us and we cry out to him, then we are raising our minds and hearts to him and he hears us. Realizing our helplessness, we fall to our knees and cry for help. Though we may not feel refreshed in such a troubled state, God's grace is already at work in us, softening our hardness of heart and shattering our self-sufficiency. "A broken and contrite heart, O God, you will not despise" (Ps 51:17).

Far from being a waste of time, prayer in such difficult times helps us to face ourselves honestly. Even if we can't let go of the doubts, fears, and responsibilities that crush us, simply to present our inability and weakness to God is to pray. In his parable our Lord told us that the publican went home justified, even though he only stood at the back of the temple, not even daring to raise his eyes to God, and begged, "God, be merciful to me, a sinner!" (Lk 18:13). To face the obstacles that hinder us from praying and bring them to the Lord is to pray. For this is to turn to God in our desperation and give him what every father wants of his child—trust. The greater our weakness, the more our trust pleases God. A greater awareness of our weakness fosters the humility required to let God take over in order to grow strong with his strength.

But this requires perseverance, like that of the Syro-Phoenician woman who wouldn't take "no" for an answer, like the desperate father who begged for faith, and like the blind beggar who cried out for a cure. God wants us to pray about the problem with persistence, continually asking God's help to resolve it. If we give the problem to him, he will help us. He has given his word: "Come to me, all you that are weary and are carrying heavy burdens, and I will give you rest. Take my yoke upon you, and learn from me; for I am gentle and humble in heart, and you will find rest for your souls" (Mt 11:28–29).

In time the doubts, distractions, and worries will cease and we will begin to "taste and see that the Lord is good" (Ps 34:8), gradually coming to realize the Lord's promise: "For surely I know the plans I have for you, says the Lord, plans for your welfare and not for harm, to give you a future with hope" (Jer 29:11). By putting our burdens at his feet and talking with him, we find the strength to shoulder them again, and our trust and confidence in him begins to grow. In time we will come to pray more eagerly, love more ardently, and rest more securely in God. Our Lord taught us this in his parable of the mustard seed, the smallest of all seeds, which grows into a tree that can shelter birds in its branches (cf. Mt 13:31–32). The seed of faith that feeds on good, rich soil needs time to grow (cf. Lk 8:8, 15). We need to pray for deeper faith and a greater spirit of prayer. Our struggle to trust God prepares the rich but hardened soil of our hearts to receive the good seed of faith. When God rains down his grace upon us, our faith and hope in him will produce an abundant harvest of the fruits of the Spirit: love, joy and peace (cf. Gal 5:22). But when we present ourselves to the Lord, we need to be patient and persevere.

The difficulties we experience in prayer can be turned into the very substance of our prayer when we offer them to God and beg for his grace to overcome them. We cannot suffer defeat when we believe in God as our Father. "Have confidence," our Lord said, "I have conquered the world" (Jn 16:33). "This is the victory that conquers the world, our faith" (1 Jn 5:4). We believe that God is our Father and that "all things work together for good for those who love God" (Rom 8:28)— even our difficulties in prayer.

foR Reflection

Rejoice in the Lord always; again I will say, Rejoice. Let your gentleness be known to everyone. The Lord is near. Do not worry about anything, but in everything by prayer and supplication with thanksgiving let your requests be made known to God. And the peace of God, which surpasses all understanding, will guard your hearts and your minds in Christ Jesus (Phil 4:4–7).

"Ask, and it will be given you; search, and you will find; knock, and the door will be opened for you. For

everyone who asks receives, and everyone who searches finds, and for everyone who knocks, the door will be opened. Is there anyone among you who, if your child asks for a fish, will give a snake instead of a fish? Or if the child asks for an egg, will give a scorpion? If you then, who are evil, know how to give good gifts to your children, how much more will the heavenly Father give the Holy Spirit to those who ask him!" (Lk 11:9–13).

What priority do I give to my prayer?

How am I allowing the Lord to lead me into deeper prayer?

What is my prayer like when I encounter difficulties? How do I share that with the Lord?

18

Celebrating the Eucharist

EVEN A SIMPLE MEAL TURNS INTO A FEAST WHEN EATEN WITH friends. We take our time over it and even lose track of time while enjoying good conversation, love, and laughter. Sometimes, however, the discussion turns to more serious matters, as we speak from the depths of our hearts. Whether our words be jovial or serious, eating a meal with friends nourishes mind and body, heart and soul.

So when Jesus established the Eucharist, he gathered his disciples around the table at the Last Supper and told them, "I have eagerly desired to eat this Passover with you before I suffer" (Lk 22:15). He spoke at length about his love for God and for them, about his life and approaching death, about his commandment of perfect love. After instituting the Eucharist he told them: "Do this in remembrance of me" (Lk 22:19). The Church has faithfully obeyed this command for two thousand years. Scripture recounts that each day the early Christians "broke bread at home and ate their food with glad and generous hearts" (Acts 2:46).

Why does the daily celebration of the Eucharist sustain a religious community as nothing else can? Vatican II said that the Eucharist is "the source and summit of the Christian life" (*Lumen Gentium, 11*). Through this memorial of Christ's passion, death, and resurrection, we offer praise and thanksgiving to the Father and recall Jesus' command to love one another as selflessly as he loved us. The Eucharist is both a sacrifice and a sacrament; it brings us into communion with God and with one another. At the Eucharist we choose the better part and sit like Mary at Christ's feet, listening to him speak to us. Then we share in Christ's own Body and Blood, which draws us into closer union. We gather as friends in the Lord and share our faith, our deepest convictions, our love for God and for one another.

These spiritual goods increase when they are shared, unlike material goods, which are used up when given away. By sharing ideas and ideals, everyone comes away enriched. We can admire and imitate those who live by great ideals, and such sharing helps good friendships to develop. When friends committed to pursuing holiness share a meal, they not only eat from the same table, they feed each other's minds and hearts by talking about the issues and concerns that bind them together. They grow more rooted in God.

At the Eucharist, Christians can share spiritual goods in the most profound way. At the first Eucharist, Jesus revealed the perfection of divine love: "For the Father himself loves you, because you have loved me and have believed that I came from God" (Jn 16:27). He spoke of his love for his disciples: "No one has greater love than this, to lay down one's life for one's friends. You are my friends if you do what I command you" (Jn 15:13–14). Jesus explained the kind of love he expects his disciples to have for one another when he said: "This is my commandment, that you love one another as I have loved you" (Jn 15:12). Even though he knew his disciples would not fully understand his words, he was laying the foundation, igniting the spark that would flame out in love when the Holy Spirit would descend on the disciples at Pentecost. At the Last Supper Jesus called his disciples his "friends" because he had made known to them everything he had heard from his father (cf. Jn 15:15). He also told us to love as he loved us, as friends.

At the Last Supper, too, Christ shared with us his own body and blood:

> Then he took a cup, and after giving thanks he said, "Take this and divide it among yourselves; for I tell you that from now on I will not drink of the fruit of the vine until the kingdom of God comes." Then he took a loaf of bread, and when he had given thanks, he broke it and gave it to them, saying, "This is my body, which is given for you. Do this in remembrance of me." And he did the same with the cup after supper, saying, "This cup that is poured out for you is the new covenant in my blood" (Lk 22:17–20).

The Eucharist brings to fruition our union with God and with one another. At the Eucharist we share the most sacred realities in our lives and experience ever deeper love, peace, and joy (cf. Jn 15:11). In the celebration of the Eucharist God's kingdom comes to earth as a foretaste of the heavenly kingdom, where we will see God as he is (cf. 1 Jn 3:2) and find perfect joy (cf. Jn 16:22) and unity.

Because the Eucharist is the sacrament of unity, Jesus asks that we forgive each other and reconcile our differences before approaching the sacred altar. For if we have closed our hearts to one another by refusing to forgive, how can we truly celebrate our oneness in the Lord? The Eucharist requires us to open our minds and hearts to God and to one another. As the source and symbol of our unity, the Eucharist leads us to true and total sharing, to communion with God and one another.

Celebrating the Eucharist with lively faith, genuine love, and profound peace and joy strengthens us in living together as friends in the Lord. So profoundly did the Eucharist affect the earliest followers of Christ that they gathered every day in their homes for the breaking of the bread (cf. Acts 2:46). Today the Lord still invites us to make it the center of our lives.

At the daily celebration of the Eucharist the word of the Lord is proclaimed, teaching us what the Gospel means in our lives. Participating in this memorial of Christ's passion and death moves us to praise and thank the Father. The Eucharist draws us closer together on the path toward the same goal—to be holy as our heavenly Father is holy. In celebrating the Eucharist we can experience not only forgiveness but genuine, heartfelt love. After receiving Communion we can spend quiet moments of peaceful prayer with Christ really present within us. This moment, the most sacred of the day, brings marvelous spiritual effects.

Our quiet thanksgiving after Holy Communion, when Christ is truly present within us, provides the time most conducive to quiet contemplation. We can enter into our hearts, pour out our love and gratitude, and earnestly entreat the Lord for our needs and those of others. During our thanksgiving Jesus invites us to draw close to him, drop our burdens at his feet, and rest in his presence. He wants us to experience what he promised the woman at the well: "Those who drink of the water that I will give them will never be thirsty. The water that I will give will become in them a spring of water gushing up to eternal life" (Jn 4:14).

When the two disciples—disappointed, discouraged, disheartened, and disbelieving—were trudging along on the road to Emmaus, Jesus appeared and walked along with them. He opened their minds to understand the Scriptures and explained why the Christ had to suffer to enter into his glory. But they came to recognize him only at the "breaking of the bread." So it is with us who are friends in the Lord and companions who follow Jesus as he leads us on the way to the Father. In the Eucharist we celebrate the presence of Jesus in our midst.

"Companion" comes from the Latin words *cum* (with) and *panis* (bread). Companions share their bread with one another. As friends in the Lord, we are also companions on our way to the Father. The Eucharist nourishes and strengthens us to continue on our way despite weakness, obstacles, and failure. The daily community celebration of the Eucharist gives us the grace, courage, and enthusiasm that we need to go forward without looking back or falling by the wayside.

This sacrament helps us realize more perfectly than at any other moment of our day our communion with God and with one another. The Eucharist reminds us of the selfless love of Christ that he calls us to imitate. It gives us a foretaste of the kingdom of God where faith will give way to vision, where we will see God as he is and find perfect love, joy, and peace.

for Reflection

Jesus said to them, "Very truly, I tell you, unless you eat the flesh of the Son of Man and drink his blood, you have no life in you. Those who eat my flesh and

drink my blood have eternal life, and I will raise
them up on the last day; for my flesh is true food
and my blood is true drink. Those who eat my flesh
and drink my blood abide in me, and I in them. Just
as the living Father sent me, and I live because of
the Father, so whoever eats me will live because of
me. This is the bread that came down from heaven,
not like that which your ancestors ate, and they
died. But the one who eats this bread will live
forever" (Jn 6:53–58).

Since, then, we have a great high priest who has
passed through the heavens, Jesus, the Son of God, let
us hold fast to our confession. For we do not have a
high priest who is unable to sympathize with our weaknesses, but we have one who in every respect has been
tested as we are, yet without sin. Let us therefore
approach the throne of grace with boldness, so that we
may receive mercy and find grace to help in time of
need (Heb 4:14–16).

Jesus gives us himself in the Eucharist. How do I in
turn make a gift of myself to others?

How can I make the Eucharistic celebration the
center of my day?

19

Apostolic Dynamism

*T*ODAY THE CHURCH GREATLY NEEDS ZEALOUS PRIESTS AND religious. For many people do not know Jesus Christ, or oppose Christianity. Some think we do not need God, because science has made such great advances. Some philosophers build up systems of thought on the assumption that God does not exist. Yet in a world that often claims God is dead, we proclaim that we believe in God. We even dare to call him "Father," and like the first apostles, we witness to the resurrection of the Lord.

Others may ridicule and oppose us, but fidelity to our holy vocation causes us to burn with a holy zeal. We need apostolic dynamism not just for a few years when new challenges excite us, but throughout our whole lives, even when the excitement wears off, youthful energy wanes, and we face difficult work. We are consecrated for mission. Referring to religious, Pope John Paul II has written: "The task of *devoting themselves wholly to 'mission'* is therefore included in their call; indeed, by the action of the Holy Spirit who is at the origin of every vocation and charism, consecrated life itself is a mission, as was the whole of Jesus' life" (*On Consecrated Life*, n. 72).

We may not think much about zeal while we are in formation, but simply assume that we have it. We have entered our communities out of zeal for God's work and concern for other human beings. Full of youthful energy and vigor, we pursue our studies, although we may prefer the active life. We generate great ideas about the liturgy, the Word of God, pastoral theology and ministry to the poor, sick, and elderly. We develop plans for youth groups, study groups, adult education, and social programs and enjoy helping in various parish activities. The active apostolate attracts us. But does all this make us zealous? Many generations of religious have assumed that they had much zeal, yet after initial bursts of creative energy, they slipped into dull routines. What happened to the zeal of their younger days? Did they ever really have it? For real virtue does not fade but grows with age.

Hope, dreams, and heroism inspire young people, who enjoy natural vitality. This buoyancy of spirit is partly physical, for a toned body makes us feel good and energetic. But zeal is not a feeling. Our youthful optimism comes partly from inexperience, which prevents us from seeing the complexity of problems and our own limitations. We can easily misjudge these purely natural factors as zeal in God's service, and when they vanish with our youth we may grow disgruntled, cynical, even bitter. Forming a truly zealous spirit now will help to avoid this.

Zeal overflows from an intense love of God and neighbor, so it has all the strength of charity. One could even say that zeal is charity in action and that our zeal measures our charity. If we love God intensely, we will be devoted to the Eucharist, to community, and to private prayer because these put us into a close personal relationship with God.

We will want to serve others and share with them the happiness we have found in our faith. As Scripture tells us, "The commandment we have from him is this: those who love God must love their brothers and sisters also" (1 Jn 4:21). Zeal spurs us to serve others out of love and inspires us to take our religious or priestly duties seriously. We will offer or participate in Mass devoutly, doing whatever we can to help people enter into Christ's sacrifice more completely. We will not rush through the liturgy but will pray reverently, knowing that our demeanor can help or hinder the devotion of others. In a priest or religious, carelessness, irreverence, or disrespect in the service of God can scandalize others. Does not Scripture tell us that Christ was heard for his reverence? (cf. Heb 5:7).

Zeal makes us eager to minister to those entrusted to us. Each of us, whether a priest, brother, or sister, needs to have a pastoral spirit, the spirit of a *pastor animarum* (shepherd of souls). A true shepherd feeds the Lord's sheep and does not merely herd them. True zeal makes us eager to study and meditate so that we will have something valuable to say when we preach, teach, or counsel others. We will take the time to prepare our lessons or homilies carefully, getting to know our people and their situations, so that we can understand them and minister to them in the trials they face.

Such a life demands great love, which exacts a great price. Perhaps we talk too much about the primacy of love and not enough about the price of love. Zealous priests, brothers, or sisters are willing and even eager to pay its high price, for love makes them prodigal. St. Augustine put it well: "Where there is love there is no labor, and if there is labor it is a labor of love." Zeal flows from charity just as light and warmth flow from fire.

St. John's Gospel recounts the incident when Christ three times asked St. Peter: "Simon, son of John, do you love me?" After Peter had three times assured him, "Lord, you know everything; you know that I love you," Jesus told him, "Feed my sheep" (Jn 21:15f.). The Gospel narrative implies that we must love Christ if we are to feed his flock. Only if we have a deep love for Christ, the whole Christ, head and members, will we care for those entrusted to us with a zeal that always grows.

I think it is extremely important to stress that priestly and religious zeal flows from charity. In our age many people question and criticize authority and institutions. Priests and religious can also be affected by this, growing angry and impatient if their views and proposals are rejected. They can then slip over the fine line between being zealous and being fanatical. Fanatics lose their perspective and easily become self-righteous, critical, and harsh. They set goals and want to achieve them immediately. They grow angry at opposition and want to force others rather than persuade them. But true zeal does not lead to such conduct.

No matter how convinced we are about the liturgy, about reform of society, education, the economy, etc., we cannot use force or be fanatics. We try to *persuade* by showing others the value of our proposals. Criticism, impatience, unkindness, and unfair pressure do not serve the cause of Christ. If we use them, even for a good cause, we are not being zealous but fanatical.

Because religious zeal springs from charity, it has all the characteristics of charity that St. Paul described. Just like charity, religious zeal "is patient...kind...not envious or boastful or arrogant or rude. It does not insist on its own way; it is not irritable or resentful; it does not rejoice in wrongdoing, but rejoices in the truth. It bears all things, believes all things, hopes all things, endures all things" (1 Cor 13:4–7). A person who follows St. Paul's advice acts in a truly selfless way. I would like to emphasize this aspect of religious zeal, its *selflessness*. For true zeal, like the charity that begets it, does not seek its own advantage. Zeal requires humility, which helps us seek God's glory and not self-satisfaction.

Christ reminded us: "Remember the word that I said to you, 'Servants are not greater than their master.' If they persecuted me, they will persecute you; if they kept my word, they will keep yours also. But they will do all these things to you on account of my name, because they do not know him who sent me" (Jn 15:20–21).

Jesus is warning us not always to expect cooperation and success in our work, but often resistance and sometimes failure, or at least apparent failure. Humanly speaking, Jesus failed miserably: he met with constant resistance from his opponents, from the crowds, and even from his uncomprehending apostles. Suffering rejection, he died an apparent failure, for the wonders of Pentecost did not occur until after Christ's death. Our Master tells us to expect the same.

To dedicate ourselves to our apostolic work under these conditions is difficult. Our Lord asks us to work with energy, vigor, and enthusiasm; to be creative and imaginative; to be patient and to persevere even though we do not see any immediate results from our work. To work zealously under these conditions requires nothing less than heroism, yet Christ asks this of us.

God will help us to rid ourselves of that very human, worldly manner of judging our efforts in terms of their success. God does not use this criterion to judge us. As Jesus said: "For here the saying holds true, 'One sows and another reaps.' I sent you to reap that for which you did not labor. Others have labored, and you have entered into their labor" (Jn 4:37–38). Our success may be due to the labors of another. St. Paul, that truly zealous apostle of the Gentiles, learned this lesson well: "I planted, Apollos watered, but God gave the growth. So neither the one who plants nor the one who waters is anything, but only God who gives the growth" (1 Cor 3:6–7).

St. Paul goes on to give the mind of a truly zealous apostle: "The one who plants and the one who waters have a common purpose" (1 Cor 3:8). Paul and his disciples worked as a team. They weren't concerned about personal success and recognition, but about service.

Then St. Paul gives us God's standard for measuring our success as ministers: "Each will receive wages according to the labor of each" (1 Cor 3:8). God uses this measure to determine our worth: how hard we worked for him. God wants our labor, our effort, our work. He will give success when it pleases him.

In our apostolic work, God counts our labor, not our success. We can't begin too soon to learn this hard lesson. Humble, selfless charity will sustain true zeal and enthusiasm. The physical vigor of youth, the natural enthusiasm that accompanies a new work, the hope of great success will vanish all too soon, like dew under the morning sun. If these alone have sustained our activity, then we will grow tepid like salt that has lost its savor, useless to the Church.

Today we need apostolic dynamism more than ever before, but trials and hardships eat away at it. Only one motive can sustain us, *charity like that of Christ*. Our zeal springs from that charity, which abides forever (cf. 1 Cor 13:13). No other motive will suffice. For true zeal will enable us to say with St. Paul, "the love of Christ urges us on" (2 Cor 5:14). True zeal expresses our selfless love for God and his people.

foR Reflection

Since it is by God's mercy that we are engaged in this ministry, we do not lose heart. We have renounced the shameful things that one hides; we refuse to practice cunning or to falsify God's word; but by the open statement of the truth we commend ourselves to the conscience of everyone in the sight of God.... For we do not proclaim ourselves; we proclaim Jesus Christ as Lord and ourselves as your slaves for Jesus' sake. For it is the God who said, "Let light shine out of darkness," who has shone in our hearts to give the light of the knowledge of the glory of God in the face of Jesus Christ. But we have this treasure in clay jars, so that it may be made clear that this extraordinary power belongs to God and does not come from us (2 Cor 4:1–2, 5–7).

If I could measure my desire to bring the love of Christ to the world, what would it be on a scale of one to ten?

What motivates me to do the work I am doing?

20

how do we glorify god?

AT THE LAST SUPPER CHRIST SAID, "MY FATHER IS GLORI-fied by this, that you bear much fruit" (Jn 15:8). St. Paul echoes this teaching when he tells us to "do everything for the glory of God" (1 Cor 10:31). But how do we give glory to God? Our praise adds nothing to his greatness (cf. Week-day Preface #4).

We value the praise of our peers who can appreciate the excellence of our work more than that of those who do not really understand it. But "who has directed the spirit of the Lord, or as his counselor has instructed him?" (Isa 40:13) How then would our feeble praise glorify God?

This issue also has a more troublesome aspect. Our Lord criticized those who did their good deeds in public so they could be seen and praised. He said they had already received their reward. But in the priestly prayer at the Last Supper, Christ prays: "Father, the hour has come; glorify your Son so that the Son may glorify you" (Jn 17:1). He told the apostles that in coming upon them the Holy Spirit "will glorify me" (Jn 16:14). No one was more selfless than Christ and to hear him praying to be glorified seems inconsistent with his life and teaching. How can we make sense of all this?

Furthermore, in St. John's Gospel Jesus refers to his passion and death as the hour of his glorification: "The hour has come for the Son of Man to be glorified" (Jn 12:27). This can puzzle us, for Jesus' passion and death might be seen as the hour of his utter humiliation. He was rejected and condemned to death, scourged, spat upon, crowned with thorns, mocked, stripped naked, and nailed to a cross between two thieves to die in agony. What kind of glory is that? In his resurrection and ascension Christ, the Son in whom the Father is well pleased (cf. Lk 3:22), indeed received the glory he had with the Father "before the world existed" (Jn 17:5). But why does Jesus speak of his utterly humiliating passion and death as glorifying his Father and himself?

"Glory" refers to the admiration and praise given to those who do great deeds. The more extraordinary the feat, the greater power it has to elicit the admiration and applause of those who view it. Athletes from around the world compete in the Olympic Games to show their skill and win a gold, silver, or bronze medal and the applause of a worldwide audience. But Christ seems to find glory in his defeat. What did he see in his passion and death to glorify himself and his Father?

St. John's Gospel gives us a clear answer: "Now before the festival of the Passover, Jesus knew that his hour had come to depart from this world and go to the Father. Having loved his own who were in the world, he loved them to the end" (Jn 13:6). The last part of this verse can be rendered, "He showed how *perfect* his love was," for the Greek term *eis telos* can mean "to the end" or "to perfection."

By his passion and death Christ revealed the perfection of his love for us. He wanted us to understand the meaning of his sacrificial death, so he told us: "No one has greater love than this, to lay down one's life for one's friends" (Jn 15:13). Jesus spent his whole life in selfless giving; his whole life revealed his selfless love and extraordinary generosity. He emptied himself, giving up the outward glory of his divinity in becoming man. He taught us about God as Father and the freedom of the Spirit; he healed the sick, comforted the sorrowing, pardoned the sinner, and forgave his enemies. He gave heaven to the good thief and gave his mother to the Church. When he had nothing else to give, he gave his spirit into the hands of his Father. The passion and death of Christ glorified him by revealing the *utter perfection of his selfless love for his Father and for us*. Because he died in obedience to his Father who "so loved the world that he gave his only Son, so that everyone who believes in him may not perish but may have eternal life" (Jn 3:16). The passion and death of Jesus also reveal the *perfection of the Father's love for us*. This is the meaning of Jesus' statement at the Last Supper after Judas had left to betray him: "Now the Son of Man has been glorified, and God has been glorified in him" (Jn 13:31), and again, "Father, the hour has come; glorify your Son so that the Son may glorify you" (Jn 17:1).

Glory, however, does not consist merely in showing one's excellence but in the admiration, love, and praise it evokes in those who can appreciate it. The apostles, however, did not yet know and appreciate the perfection of divine love, for at first the passion and death of Christ dismayed them. They found Christ's death ignominious, not glorious. Like the disciples on the road to Emmaus, who had to be taught why it was "necessary that the Messiah should suffer these things and then enter into his glory" (Lk 24:26), the apostles did not appreciate what Christ had done. Nor would they until the Holy Spirit came upon them. Only with the Holy Spirit's help would the apostles and disciples realize and appreciate the meaning of Christ's passion and death. Then they could glorify God on account of his great love. Christ had promised them at the Last Supper: "When the Spirit of truth comes, he will guide you into all the truth.... He will glorify me, because he will take what is mine and declare it to you. All that the Father has is mine" (Jn 16:13–15).

Christ came that we might know and worship the Father "in spirit and truth" (Jn 4:24). Jesus wanted to spread the good news of the mystery of divine love and told the apostles: "I do as the Father has commanded me, so that the world may know that I love the Father" (Jn 14:31). Christ has revealed his love for the Father and entrusted that revelation to us, his disciples. He has also told us *how* we are to show this divine love to the world: "I give you a new commandment, that you love one another. Just as I have loved you, you also should love one another. *By this every-one will know that you are my disciples, if you have love for one another*" (Jn 13:34–35; emphasis added).

By dying on the cross in obedience to his Father's will, Jesus revealed the perfect love he and the Father have for each other and for us. If we love one another as Christ has loved us, our unselfish love can inspire those who see it to say, "Look how these Christians love one another." It can draw them to know and love God too. Thus we not only glorify God by the love *we* give to him and to our neighbor in imitation of Christ, we also bring *others* to glorify God too. In so doing we fulfill the commission Christ gave us to bear "fruit that will last" (Jn 15:16). For we glorify God in bearing much fruit (cf. Jn 15:8), especially the fruit of love.

God wants to unite all of us with him by love. For as the Church teaches, God created the world freely, to share his goodness with us. We will find perfect fulfillment only in our union with him in perfect love in heaven, when we will see him as he is and God's glory will fully shine.

Just as star differs from star in glory (cf. 1 Cor 15:41) so do the saints in heaven. Imitating God's selfless love for us, we prepare ourselves for the glory of heaven by the perfection of our love here on earth. The more we can empty ourselves of self-seeking and grow in unselfish love for God and each other, the more room we make for God's love to fill us, and the more we will manifest the glory of God, the perfection of his love in us.

St. Paul wants us to draw this lesson from the life and death of Jesus:

> Let the same mind be in you that was in Christ Jesus,
>
> who, though he was in the form of God,
>
> did not regard equality with God
>
> as something to be exploited,
>
> but emptied himself,
>
> taking the form of a slave,
>
> being born in human likeness.
>
> And being found in human form,
>
> he humbled himself
>
> and became obedient to the point of death—
>
> even death on a cross.
>
> *Therefore God also highly exalted him*
>
> *and gave him the name*
>
> *that is above every name,*
>
> *so that at the name of Jesus*
>
> *every knee should bend,*
>
> *in heaven and on earth and under the earth,*

and every tongue should confess

that Jesus Christ is Lord,

to the glory of God the Father (Phil 2:5–1 1; emphasis added).

The Christian conception of glory resolves all the paradoxes referred to earlier. The glory of God the Father, the glory of Christ, and our own eternal glory are all joined together in perfect love. For by his life and death Christ revealed to us the kind of love God gives to us and expects of us, love that is like his own, absolutely selfless, pure benevolence. Christ also taught us that God is a loving Father who sent his Son and his Holy Spirit to draw all of us into the circle of his divine love. We glorify God by the selfless love we give to him and to one another. This is why St. Paul can say: "It can only be to God's glory, then, for you to treat each other in the same friendly way as Christ treated you" (Rom 15:7–JB), and why we earnestly pray: "Glory be to the Father, and to the Son, and to the Holy Spirit as it was in the beginning, is now and will be forever. Amen."

for Reflection

God chose to make known how great among the Gentiles are the riches of the glory of this mystery, which is Christ in you, the hope of glory. It is he whom we proclaim, warning everyone and teaching everyone in all wisdom, so that we may present everyone mature

*in Christ. For this I toil and struggle with all the energy
that he powerfully inspires within me (Col 1:27–29).*

*Whoever speaks must do so as one speaking the
very words of God; whoever serves must do so with the
strength that God supplies, so that God may be glorified in all things through Jesus Christ. To him belong
the glory and the power forever and ever. Amen.*

*Beloved, do not be surprised at the fiery ordeal that
is taking place among you to test you, as though something strange were happening to you. But rejoice insofar as you are sharing Christ's sufferings, so that you
may also be glad and shout for joy when his glory is
revealed. If you are reviled for the name of Christ, you
are blessed, because the spirit of glory, which is the
Spirit of God, is resting on you (1 Pet 4:11–14).*

How do I seek to glorify God in the daily events of
my life?

Do I seek to understand how the sufferings I experience are related to glory?

21

the perfection of Charity: heaven

WE ARE RESTLESS CREATURES WHO LIVE OUR LIVES WITH longing, searching for fulfillment and happiness. While working to complete a project, we anticipate the joy of finishing it. Children dream of the day when they will go to college and earn a degree, while parents want to see their children grown up and settled. And so it goes. We live our lives expecting and hoping for happiness to come.

Why do this? It's not because the present is unbearable, but because nothing we experience completely fulfills us. Something may momentarily satisfy our desires, but then new cravings arise. Some beauty may delight us, then after that brief interlude our quest continues.

This indicates that God made us for better things, destined for greater joys than this world offers. Our faith tells us that God has made us for himself and that we will find eternal happiness only in him. St. Augustine was right when he said: "You have made us for yourself, O Lord, and our hearts are restless until they rest in thee."

Even so, we may have ambiguous feelings about heaven, feeling like the old bishop who had worn himself out with work. The doctor examined him carefully, then shook his head and said, "Bishop, you need rest desperately. I'm giving you an alternative. Either go on vacation for a month or get ready to go to heaven." The bishop went on vacation.

The thought of Christ's second coming may not fill us with joy because we fear the calamities that the Gospels say will precede his coming. But why fear them? Scripture says that when we see all the signs in the sun, moon, and stars, we should stand up straight and lift our heads because our redemption has drawn near (cf. Lk 21:28). As the psalmist says: "Even though I walk through the darkest valley, I fear no evil; for you are with me" (Ps 23:4). Christ's second coming will renew the world rather than destroy it. The old world will be swept away, transformed by the fire of the divine love that Christ has cast upon the earth.

Nor should the thought of God's judgment frighten us, for Jesus has told us, "The Father judges no one but has given all judgment to the Son" (Jn 5:22). Christ has told us, "I came not to judge the world but to save the world. The one who rejects me and does not receive my word has a judge; *on the last day the word that I have spoken will serve as judge*" (Jn 12:47–48; emphasis added). Our final judgment will reveal how well we have fulfilled the Lord's command: "Love one another as I have loved you" (Jn 15:12). The final judgment will consist in the revelation of our love. For love like Christ's does not keep score of wrongs. There is no need to, because our love will reveal how much or how little good we have done. For sin is selfishness, and only sin can prevent God's love from entering our hearts and producing fruit that will last. Jesus has told us: "Those who love me will keep my word, and my Father will love them, and we will come to them and make our home with them" (Jn 14:23). This love casts out fear, as John tells us:

We have come to know and to believe in the love God has for us. God is love, and whoever remains in love remains in God and God in him.

In this is love brought to perfection among us, that we have confidence on the day of judgment because as he is, so are we in this world.

There is no fear in love, but *perfect love drives out fear* because fear has to do with punishment, and so one who fears is not yet perfect in love (1 Jn 4:16–18–JB; emphasis added).

Nor should our natural fear of death overcome us, for God will give us the grace to accept death willingly and to face it with strength. It is our final sacrifice, the moment when we can give back to God our whole life with its failures and successes, its hidden labors and sacrifices, its joys and sorrows — we give all this to God with love and gratitude. Death opens for us the gateway to glory.

Our love of God casts out all morbid fear of death and judgment and frees us to think about heaven, the goal of every Christian. What will heaven be like? In heaven we will experience perfect joy. It has no place for sorrow, temptations, sin, anguish, or remorse. After the final resurrection, we will enjoy a wonderful harmony in our souls and bodies. Heaven will see the end of strife and struggle; it will banish doubt, worry, and fear; it will lift forever the cruel pressures that weigh so heavily upon us now. Nothing will disappoint us. Heaven knows no discord, no conflicts. We will enjoy perfect union with those we love, never fearing death, which Christ has conquered forever. Heaven means the end of all our sufferings and the beginning of unending joy.

We can hardly imagine the delights heaven has in store for us. Artists have tried to picture heaven for us using Scriptural imagery, but they can convey only a faint idea of it. Mosaics in the old churches of Rome often portray Christ seated on an elaborate throne, surrounded by the twenty-four elders clothed like Roman senators in white tunics, kneeling with heads bent low in adoration. Although this makes for beautiful liturgical symbolism, reminding us that the Church on earth unites its voice with the heavenly hosts, these mosaics hardly convey the intensity of heaven's joys.

But we need not rely on these images to form an idea of heaven. Scripture is quite explicit. For example, our Lord said: "This is eternal life, that they may know you, the only true God, and Jesus Christ whom you have sent" (Jn 17: 3). St. Paul has written: "Now we see in a mirror, dimly, but then we will see face to face" (1 Cor 13:12). The First Letter of John says: "See what love the Father has given us, that we should be called children of God; and that is what we are.... Beloved, we are God's children now; what we will be has not yet been revealed. What we do know is this: when he is revealed, we will be like him, for we will see him as he is" (1 Jn 3:2). Scripture clearly states that the joy and glory of heaven will consist in seeing God face to face and being made like him in that vision. That will be our eternal happiness.

Does this sound exciting? Probably not. Perhaps we imagine heaven as a movie, a stupendous super-colossal spectacle, the show to end all shows, with ourselves staring wide-eyed and open-mouthed as the divine essence reveals itself. Heaven will not be like that either. We will see God as he is, but we will not look at him as though he were outside of us. God is a pure spirit whom we cannot see with our bodily eyes. This need not astonish us. Even in this life we know the love our friends have for us, but we cannot see love. Perhaps it is better to speak of being keenly aware of

God's presence within us and of his tender love for us rather than of seeing him. For if in our earthly life when we must walk by faith, "this is how we know that we remain in him and he in us, that he has given us of his Spirit" (1 Jn 4:13). In heaven God will take us to himself, giving us the perfect love we have always wanted, so we can rest in his fatherly embrace. We will live in him, always aware of his presence, overjoyed at his beauty, ever grateful for his love.

We cannot form an adequate idea of what God's beauty will be like, nor of the intense joy it will evoke in us. But we do know from the beauty of his creation that God himself is supremely beautiful and good. We enjoy hearing the laughter of a child and the song of a bird, or seeing a fluffy cloud float across a clear sky. Think of the majesty of the mountains, the immensity of the ocean, the splendor of a starry night, and blazing sunsets. Their beauty moves us deeply, although we may not all have the poet's facility to articulate our feelings. Who can describe even one sunset adequately? The sun has been setting for millions of years, yet its beauty is never exhausted.

Think too of the pleasure we get from people: the innocence, simplicity, and trust of a child, the tenderness and love of a mother, the constant, kindly, gentle concern of a father. All these things delight us. So do our friends. Each has special qualities that attract us: kindness, warmth, sympathy, cheerfulness, buoyancy, spontaneity, good temper, generosity. All our friends have beauty of character and special charm, each in a unique way.

So many things give us pleasure in this world, yet the beauty of nature can never satisfy us. Nor should it, for it is meant to draw us to the source of all beauty, God. As the psalmist says, "The heavens are telling the glory of God; and the firmament proclaims his handiwork" (Ps 19:1). All the finite, limited perfections of nature reveal to us something of God's perfection. The beauty we find here is found in God in a more perfect way, eminently, transcendently, but with this difference. Here on earth beauty is incomplete and limited, but in God it is complete and perfect. It would be like seeing the beauty of all the sunsets from the beginning to the end of time in one single view. It would be like finding the beauty of every face, the virtue of every friend in one person. For God is absolutely perfect and supremely beautiful.

We are made for the vision of God. Because God is our goal, our purpose, he alone can satisfy us. But will we ever tire of God? Eternity never ends, so can we have too much of a good thing? No! Not in this case, for God is infinite. We will never penetrate the depths, never exhaust the wonders of his beauty, for he is "beauty ever old and ever new" (St. Augustine).

In heaven, too, we will enjoy the presence of Christ, Mary, and all the saints. By "saints" I mean all our friends, all of us. We will have all the joys of our human friendships unspoiled by human imperfection. God's beauty and holiness will transform us all, thus enhancing our joy in being with each other.

Recall how joy or excitement can transfigure a person, how a flash of understanding can light up a student's face, how a feeling of tenderness and pity can soften a face ravaged by work and worry. Think of holy persons who radiate joy, peace, and the presence of God. But we can hardly imagine how the vision of God will transform us, when no selfishness will prevent God's glory from shining through us. Yes, "the faithful [shall] exult in glory; let them sing for joy" (Ps 149:5).

In speaking of our future glory, however, I do not wish to imply that we will walk among the heavenly hosts proudly displaying our dazzling beauty. Not at all, for heaven is for the humble of heart. There we will see clearly that ours is a reflected beauty like that of the moon, which shines with light reflected from the sun. We will understand clearly that we have been saved through the grace Christ won for us by his death, and we will see what God has achieved in us through our selfless love. At last we will be able to make Mary's prayer our own: "My soul proclaims the greatness of the Lord; my spirit rejoices in God my savior. For he has looked upon his handmaid's lowliness; behold, from now on will all ages call me blessed" (Lk 1:46–49).

But we have to face one final nagging issue. We contemplate the glories of heaven to encourage us on our earthly pilgrimage. St. Paul reminds us that "the sufferings of this present time are as nothing compared with the glory to be revealed for us" (Rom 8:18). But if we strive for holiness so as to enter the glory of heaven, how can we claim that our love for God is selfless? *Does not our very desire and hope for eternal glory make our love self-seeking and mercenary? Are we not then serving God for the rewards that we hope to gain from him and not out of pure benevolent love?* Certainly not! Did not Christ himself on the eve of his passion pray to be glorified with the glory he had before the world began? (cf. Jn 17:5) And who was more selfless than Christ? Just as by nature we *must* seek our own happiness — we cannot directly choose unhappiness, though we might be mistaken about what will bring us happiness — so by faith we *must* seek eternal happiness. This is God's decree.

The hope of eternal glory and the Lord's command of selfless love do not contradict each other. Reflection on a simple childhood experience can make this clear. When I was in grammar school, the sisters who taught us would put a gold star on our test papers if we got 100%. I remember one occasion running home after school clutching my gold-starred paper, eager to show it to my mother. I wasn't looking for praise, but I knew how pleased she would be with my success. I would stand before her seeing the smile on her face, exulting that I had brought her joy. That childhood experience, I think, in a way captures the joy of the blessed in heaven. For we will stand before God knowing our failures and weakness, but also aware of the good that his grace has wrought in and through us. To hear God say to us, "Well done, my good and faithful servant" (Mt 25:21), and to *know that our heavenly Father is pleased with us,* will fill us with the deepest joy. When we enter the kingdom God has prepared for us from the foundation of the world, we will experience "what eye has not seen, and ear has not heard, and what has not entered the human heart, what God has prepared for those who love him" (1 Cor 2:9), and will rejoice knowing that God has prepared all this for us because we *love* him.

foR Reflection

Do not store up for yourselves treasures on earth, where moth and rust consume and where thieves break in and steal; but store up for yourselves treasures in heaven, where neither moth nor rust consumes and where thieves do not break in and steal. For where your treasure is, there your heart will be also (Mt 6:19–21).

So we do not lose heart. Even though our outer nature is wasting away, our inner nature is being renewed day by day. For this slight momentary affliction is preparing us for an eternal weight of glory beyond all measure, because we look not at what can be seen but at what cannot be seen; for what can be seen is temporary, but what cannot be seen is eternal (2 Cor 4:16–18).

How does my life show that I live in hope of eternal life?

On what is my heart set?

22

mary, our mother

FROM THE CROSS JESUS ENTRUSTED HIS MOTHER, MARY, TO the care of St. John (cf. Jn 19:25–27). John's Gospel mentions Mary only twice, at the beginning of Christ's public life and at the end. But those two significant appearances deserve careful consideration.

Mary first appears at the wedding feast at Cana. The evangelist had previously described John's witness to Christ, how John the Baptist baptized Jesus, and the calling of the first disciples. The Gospel speaks of two disciples who followed Christ and spent the day with him. Since the details included in the account suggest it comes from an eyewitness, possibly one of the "two disciples" was John himself. The other was Andrew, who recruited his brother, Peter. The next day Jesus called a friend of Andrew and Peter named Philip, who in turn brought Nathaniel. "Three days" after the calling of the first disciples a marriage feast was held at Cana, where Jesus turned water into wine "and his disciples believed in him" (Jn 2:11).

John's narrative telescopes all these events into one week. The other Gospels, however, tell us that after his baptism Christ spent forty days in the desert before returning to Galilee where he called Peter and Andrew, James and John. Considering the time it would take to walk on the difficult terrain, it seems likely that Jesus had been away from Nazareth for a long time, so Mary must have wanted to see and talk with him again. As she traveled from Nazareth to Cana, she must have eagerly anticipated meeting Jesus.

When the wine ran out, Mary approached Jesus quietly and said, "They have no wine" (Jn 2:3). Mary clearly felt concerned about the newlyweds' embarrassment and asked Jesus to help them. He responded in an unusual way: "Woman, what concern is that to you and to me? My hour has not yet come" (Jn 2:4).

The original Greek text literally means "What is it to me and to you?" and could be translated "What concern is it to you and me?" But both Jesus and Mary would care about the embarrassment of the couple. The translation that best suits the context is "What bond is there between you and me (that you should ask me that)?" Christ seems to be distancing himself from his mother by this reply. To emphasize the point he calls her "woman," an unusual form of address.

The synoptic Gospels support this interpretation. For whenever his mother appears during Christ's public life, he diverts attention away from her physical motherhood, as the following incident shows.

> While he was still speaking to the crowds, his mother and his brothers were standing outside, wanting to speak to him. Someone told him, "Look, your mother and your brothers are standing outside, wanting to speak to you." But to the one who had told him this, Jesus replied, "Who is my mother, and who are my brothers?" And pointing to his disciples, he said, "Here are my mother and my brothers! For whoever does the will of my Father in

heaven is my brother and sister and mother" (Mt 12:46–50; cf. Mk 3:31–35; Lk 8:19–21).

On another occasion when a woman in the crowd raised her voice and cried out, "Blessed is the womb that bore you and the breasts that nursed you!" Jesus replied, "Blessed rather are those who hear the word of God and obey it!" (Lk 11:27–28).

Jesus distanced himself from his mother during his public life because he had to reveal himself to his disciples as the Son of God, and they already knew he was the son of Mary. Pope John Paul II has pointed out in his encyclical *Mother of the Redeemer* that Christ wished "to divert attention from motherhood understood only as a fleshly bond, in order to direct it toward those mysterious bonds of the spirit which develop from hearing and keeping God's word" (n. 20).

Mary listened to and kept God's word in the highest degree, which is why the Gospels agree with the woman who called Jesus' mother "blessed." At the annunciation the angel witnessed to Mary's blessedness when he called her "full of grace," the one who had won God's favor, and that because the Holy Spirit would overshadow her, her child would be holy, the Son of God (cf. Lk 1:28–33). Elizabeth too said of Mary, "Blessed are you among women, and blessed is the fruit of your womb" (Lk 1:42). The unnamed woman in the crowd echoed the praise that others in the synoptic Gospels had given to the Mother of Jesus.

At Cana, Mary's response to Jesus' apparent rejection of her request indicates the depth of understanding between Jesus and his mother. She had carried him for nine months, given him birth, nursed him, and nurtured him through childhood and adolescence. She and Joseph had shaped his character in the years when he "was obedient to them"

(Lk 2:51). She understood her son as no other human being could. She confidently told the workers, "Do whatever he tells you." Through her intercession God provided a greater abundance of far better wine than the couple ever could have provided.

Jesus' words to his mother at Cana resonate with a meaning that becomes clearer later in John's Gospel. For when he said to her, "What is that to me and to you, woman?", he added, "My hour has not yet come." He seems to imply that when *his hour* came, the true greatness of the special bond between him and his mother would stand out. What "hour" does Jesus speak of? In John's Gospel the word "hour" always refers to Christ's passion and death. After his triumphant entry into Jerusalem, knowing he would soon suffer and die, Jesus said: "The *hour* has come for the Son of Man to be glorified" (Jn 12:23). John uses the word again when he begins his account of the Last Supper: "Jesus knew that his *hour* had come to depart from this world and go to the Father. Having loved his own who were in the world, he loved them to the end" (Jn 13:1).

"The hour" refers to Christ's passion and death—"the hour" that Jesus had spoken of at Cana, implying that when his "hour" had come, the special bond between him and his mother would clearly stand out. Mary makes her second appearance in John's Gospel at the foot of the cross:

> Standing near the cross of Jesus were his mother, and his mother's sister, Mary the wife of Clopas, and Mary Magdalene. When Jesus saw his mother and the disciple whom he loved standing beside her, he said to his mother, "Woman, here is your son." Then he said to the disciple, "Here is your mother." And from that hour the disciple took her into his own home (Jn 19:25–27).

Because John's Gospel cites several passages from the Old Testament as having been fulfilled in the passion and death of Christ, some scholars think that when Jesus uses the unusual term "woman" when speaking from the cross, it has special biblical significance. Christ indicates that Mary, the lowly and faithful servant of the Lord, the new Eve, is the spiritual mother of all the faithful, here represented by the beloved disciple who from that moment took her as his own mother. This was the special relationship that Christ implied at Cana.[1]

We see here, too, how the Gospels of Luke and John complement each other. Luke calls Mary "blessed" because of her faith, which led to her being the Mother of the Lord. In John's Gospel the bond uniting Jesus and his mother extends to all those who through their faith become members of Jesus' Mystical Body. That body was formed when water and blood, symbolic of Baptism and the Eucharist, gushed from the pierced side of Christ, the sacrificial Lamb of God. Luke portrays Mary as the *model* of all believers, while John presents her as the *mother* of all believers. At the foot of the cross Mary's spiritual motherhood took on a universal dimension.

But why did Mary become Mother of the Church at this moment? The Letter to the Hebrews, which speaks of Jesus' redemptive sufferings, offers us an insight into Mary's role on Calvary: "It was fitting that God...in bringing many children to glory, should make the pioneer of their salvation perfect through sufferings" (Heb 2:10). By his suffering and

---

1. For a discussion of scholarly views about the significance of the term "woman," see Raymond Brown et al., *Mary in the New Testament: A Collaborative Assessment by Protestant and Roman Catholic Scholars* (Philadelphia: Fortress Press, 1978), pp. 188–190.

death, Christ became "like his brothers and sisters in every respect, so that he might be a merciful and faithful high priest in the service of God, to make a sacrifice of atonement for the sins of the people" (Heb 2:17). Though Son of God and absolutely sinless, as the Son of Man he had to suffer. For in his passion and death he showed the perfect love he had for his Father, and his love and compassion for us. Jesus' proof of his perfect love should enable us to "approach the throne of grace with boldness, so that we may receive mercy and find grace to help in time of need" (Heb 4:16).

Just as Christ died on the cross in obedience to his Father's will, giving us an undeniable proof of his divine love, so Mary stood at the foot of the cross in loving submission and total surrender to God's will. She accepted in faith her son's agonizing death. Without bitterness, hatred, revenge, or self-pity, she loved even those who brought about his death. Mary, like Jesus, was "made perfect through suffering." She, too, had to reveal the perfection of her motherly love and compassion for *all* of us, her sinful children. At the foot of the cross, when the sword of sorrow foretold by Simeon pierced her heart, she achieved the goal Christ set for all of us. As far as humanly possible, she became compassionate, even as our heavenly Father is compassionate (cf. Lk 6:36). During her greatest sorrow she showed the perfection of her love, and Christ made her Mother of the Church, our Blessed Mother.

Calvary revealed the depth of her love and compassion for us. Cana shows us her motherly solicitude and the power of her intercession. What more could the Gospels say about her to encourage us to approach her in all our needs with childlike confidence and love? She is truly *our Blessed Mother*.

for Reflection

In the sixth month the angel Gabriel was sent by God to a town in Galilee called Nazareth, to a virgin engaged to a man whose name was Joseph, of the house of David. The virgin's name was Mary. And he came to her and said, "Greetings, favored one! The Lord is with you." But she was much perplexed by his words and pondered what sort of greeting this might be. The angel said to her, "Do not be afraid, Mary, for you have found favor with God. And now, you will conceive in your womb and bear a son, and you will name him Jesus. He will be great, and will be called the Son of the Most High, and the Lord God will give to him the throne of his ancestor David. He will reign over the house of Jacob forever, and of his kingdom there will be no end." Mary said to the angel, "How can this be, since I am a virgin?" The angel said to her, "The Holy Spirit will come upon you, and the power of the Most High will overshadow you; therefore the child to be born will be holy; he will be called Son of God. And now, your relative Elizabeth in her old age has also conceived a son; and this is the sixth month for her who was said to be barren. For nothing will be impossible with God" (Lk 1:26–37).

What does Mary's example of willing cooperation with God say to me about my own faith response?

How do I welcome Mary into my life? What can she teach me about being a disciple of Jesus?

BOOKS & MEDIA

The Daughters of St. Paul operate book and media centers at the following addresses. Visit, call or write the one nearest you today, or find us on the World Wide Web, www.pauline.org

CALIFORNIA
3908 Sepulveda Blvd, Culver City, CA 90230   310-397-8676
5945 Balboa Avenue, San Diego, CA 92111   858-565-9181
46 Geary Street, San Francisco, CA 94108   415-781-5180

FLORIDA
145 S.W. 107th Avenue, Miami, FL 33174   305-559-6715

HAWAII
1143 Bishop Street, Honolulu, HI 96813   808-521-2731
Neighbor Islands call: 800-259-8463

ILLINOIS
172 North Michigan Avenue, Chicago, IL 60601   312-346-4228

LOUISIANA
4403 Veterans Memorial Blvd, Metairie, LA 70006   504-887-7631

MASSACHUSETTS
Rte. 1, 885 Providence Hwy, Dedham, MA 02026   781-326-5385

MISSOURI
9804 Watson Road, St. Louis, MO 63126   314-965-3512

NEW JERSEY
561 U.S. Route 1, Wick Plaza, Edison, NJ 08817   732-572-1200

NEW YORK
150 East 52nd Street, New York, NY 10022   212-754-1110
78 Fort Place, Staten Island, NY 10301   718-447-5071

OHIO
2105 Ontario Street, Cleveland, OH 44115   216-621-9427

PENNSYLVANIA
9171-A Roosevelt Blvd, Philadelphia, PA 19114   215-676-9494

SOUTH CAROLINA
243 King Street, Charleston, SC 29401   843-577-0175

TENNESSEE
4811 Poplar Avenue, Memphis, TN 38117   901-761-2987

TEXAS
114 Main Plaza, San Antonio, TX 78205   210-224-8101

VIRGINIA
1025 King Street, Alexandria, VA 22314   703-549-3806

CANADA
3022 Dufferin Street, Toronto, Ontario, Canada M6B 3T5   416-781-9131
1155 Yonge Street, Toronto, Ontario, Canada M4T 1W2   416-934-3440

¡También somos su fuente para libros, videos y música en español!